NICI

SUBDUED ANTHEMS: BACK CATALOGUE, VOLUME 1

FIERY HEDGE POETRY

SUBDUED ANTHEMS: BACK CATALOGUE, VOLUME 1

First published 2015 by Fiery Hedge Publications

ISBN 978-0-9930473-2-9

Cover design by Nick Ware assisted by Lewes Epps with photography by Chris Ware

Printed by CreateSpace

Acknowledgements

I am grateful to the editors of the following for publishing versions of some of these poems:

Belmont Focus
iota
juju
Otter
Pennine Platform
SIBBS
Weyfarers

Hedgehog House Publications released pamphlet versions of the following between 2002 and 2010:

For the Season
The Hedgehog House
The Songs of Exile
Dismantling No Man's Land
Personal Effects

Albeit inexactly, in this collection, the sequencing of these titles reflects their original order of conception and completion.

In 2013, Andrew Sparke kindly included *Where You Are* (*Dismantling No Man's Land*) with additional commentary explaining its context in his debut collection *Broken English*.

Nick Ware

SUBDUED ANTHEMS: BACK CATALOGUE, VOLUME 1

Contents

THE SONGS OF EXILE

To Chris, Kathryn, Matthew and David – who sweeten exile – and in memory of Tim Ware

How can we sing the songs of the Lord
while in a foreign land?
PSALM 137:4

After dark, I sang and played the harmonica without worrying about anything – there was no one else for miles.
TIM WARE: UNPUBLISHED TRAVEL DIARY – AUSTRALIA AND TASMANIA

BIRTH DAY

to Kathryn Amy, b. February 10th, 1989

Even then, I could sense (beneath the pure
joy in your coming, that day miracled
into our sight) the shock – as of one keel-hauled
meeting the harsh light, this expanse of air.
It takes a whole lifetime to recover
fully: touch heals, but at once you're cradled
differently, feel love holding back a world
as cold as the delivery room floor.

The first expulsion: we all come down
the same road. Behind, Zion and Eden
gape in the memory – its ancestral wound
yours, mine, everyone's, since the gulf opened
and willed in us this separation.
We are born lost – life's the search to be found.

HOMAGE

to Tim Ware, d. April 20th, 1992

You claimed once to have heard the songs of angels.
I missed that joyous portent, but the light
your gaze held then mirrored the Infinite.
Years on, it was your music stirred the dells
beneath the southern stars – on what impulse
gifted? Though here it's clay we interpret,
the voice that startled the Tasmanian night
must soar among the angels somewhere else.

And I will probe the heart's dim recesses
for echoes of that music (now withdrawn,
like you, into a yet impenetrable
silence), sing a broken rendition
– these lays the subdued anthems of the place,
the time. I will call them the songs of exile.

PERSONAL QUEST

I inhabit the past,
return time after time,
like the murderer
to the scene of a crime;

with my yellowing chart,
tread the long road back
to the dark defiles
where I missed the track;

and – at every turn
of the echoing maze –
meet some ghost of myself
in those former days,

so that ghost follows ghost
as my years unfold.
I must touch their hurt
to escape their hold,

roving back, always back,
till I chance on the key
which will unlock the past
that inhabits me.

ASKING EVE

Generations off, we stand with you
under the Tree of Good and Evil:
we see your arm trace the hanging bough,
caress it. Mother! Mother of all

that live, that die – in that moment of
ill-advised capitulation,
did you know we perish on the curve
that looks back always to the Garden?

CHILDHOOD

Innocence? More a tranquil unconcern
with outcomes – the game all, until we learn
that guilt's our natural state and the good end
one never universally attained,
though we play on.

                                        Under the chestnuts there
always were shadows. Running through the park,
sunward, we didn't notice, didn't care;
squinted towards the light, trusting, half-blind;
not thinking that our souls moved in the dark,
till branches threw dark clouds over the mind
and – two small boys passing the empty school
near summer's end – we sensed the downward pull.

BEYOND RECALL

Once – in Mid-Wales –
at the coast, I saw
a teddy bear left
by the sea-wall.

Though I moved on,
somehow the teddy's
stuck with me
ever since then.

Was he
remembered?
Did the child get there
before the tide?

I wonder
and worry.
I worry
and think

that *I*, maybe, mislaid something
years ago, but
– for the life within me –
I can't imagine what.

Borth, Dyfed

PARTY SIREN

More than the giddy air, it is the blood
carries the message, singing in the veins
– the pull of it as vast as oceans,
your untried vessel pitching on the flood.
Though the mast's near on which you might make good
your passage hence, yet her body beckons
alluringly, those dazzling cliffs advance,
and worthier goals are wildly disavowed.

Lured to her room, that dark shore's where you spill.
She, sighing over, shakes her flowing locks
then croons the ancient song. Its music charms
to oblivion, almost, lulls and lilts, until
you neither know your ship grinds on the rocks,
nor care that you have foundered in her arms.

EXILE: SECOND GENERATION

Born to its dazzling corridors of stone,
their towering heraldries – bull, dragon, lion –
these eyes see only potent Babylon,
afford the mind no memoried glimpse of Zion.

Beneath the poplars, by the Euphrates,
moulder the harps those eastbound deportees
hung there in silence above wharf and quay;
and yet my song echoes theirs distantly.

FOR THE RECORD (LOVE POEM)

to Christine

I was trying to put
my life in order, but

you found me out – my room
tidy, tucked away from

sight. You opened the door,
window, every drawer;

drew forth secrets only
you could discover. I

love you, your disturbance
of my neat arrangements.

I know, if I should lose
your love, I'd miss the mess.

FIRST BORN

Returning from the hospital
on the third night of parenthood
to the dark house in want of all
so soon to make it home, I wept,
unburdening in solitude
the untold griefs my spirit kept.

Convulsed, I thought, *their angels in*
heaven behold the Father's face;
embraced that other world unseen,
its myriad guardians hovering;
then understood – I was no less
dependent than that little thing

left with its mother on the ward.
I sensed within myself the child
crumpling up in the arms of God
as the birth pitched towards a shaft
where lifelong truths lay paralleled:
fathering, fathered; loving, loved.

POEMS FOR THE MEDIA AGE

1. TRUTH AND LIES

They say the camera never lies.
They say the artist is the product
of society.
They say this is how things are,
it is their duty to reflect
this age, these times.
Do not adjust your set
– reality defers
to the messages it sends.
They say the camera never lies,
for therein
lies the truth.

2. MEDIA MAN

Made once
in the image of God,
he is cut, spliced
and spooled
in the image of the lens.

3. TRANSMISSION

You only get out
what you put in.

It's on the street,
if it's on the screen.

4. "WE INTERRUPT THIS PROGRAMME…"

He is out there somewhere,
as you watch your screen aghast.
He is out there somewhere,
bringing the horror to life.
The lawlessness has increased
since he first roamed beyond the set.
Keep the door on its chain
(you've seen what he does to his victims!)
Do not venture outside
(you know that he's somewhere nearby,
menacing, lurking!)
Like the ghost under the bed,
like the monster beneath the stairs,
he is always waiting.
He is the self-made man
and he's coming to get you,
he's coming to get you,
he's coming to

THE EARTHBOUND TRAVELLER

To buy a simple canvas bag,
pack only the necessities
(book, change of clothes, dish, spoon and mug,
paper and pen): I could do this,

leave home without a backward look
at all the stuff I hurled behind
– the costly comforts I forsook
to rove leaf-light on any wind –

but that I'd miss the ewe-cropped grass
of chalk escarpments, winds astride
white equine figures raised there as
emblems to a whole countryside;

the downland farms, the long descent
through archetypal villages,
the fertile vale's broad testament
of churchyards, meadows, waterways;

and miss the steadfast Roman road,
bearing new motored chariots on
over the northern plain bestrewed
with settlements of honeyed stone.

I'd miss them as the weald and woods
of Surrey – its green summer lanes,
the hillside hangers (bluebell clouds
drifting the strong roots' permanence) –

or, shifting to more open ground,
that misty view of Oxford's spire-
emblazoned skyline and, around,
its gently undulating shire.

The place, no matter where, demands
some portion of the heart for rent,
so keenly I have loved the lands
of each successive banishment:

loved to my cost, since well I know
that beauty's barbed – to snag, to snare –
and every time I make to go
something inside me seems to tear.

Wiltshire

SOJOURNS

It's afterwards we grow wistful,
view the past with nostalgia,
forgetting how there also
anxiety stalked, would grip
the heart in an unguarded moment.

It's the backward look towards nightfall
recalls some golden era
among those distant hills
the sunset mellows, till hardship
is made to seem inconsequential.

And the places we abandon
are the ones internalised
on the mind's landscape – sojourns
revisited now the measure
of the present halt, its troubles.

It's the joy not then discerned
that hindsight reckons dearest,
engendering mournful notions
that the blessing comes mostly unlooked-for
and always somewhere else.

TIME AND EMOTION STUDY

The earth spins
and we with it;
only the heart
lags hopelessly behind.

THOSE EYES

in memoriam Tim Ware, 1964-1992

Those eyes are closed – eyes that once gazed upon
wonders and marvels lodged in time and space –
and we must mourn the chance that's overthrown
the mind that animated so the face,

the features, dear to memory and beheld
there only now; though, in another sense,
those eyes are open in some other world
ours will not find, till death conducts us thence.

COMING TO TERMS

for Tim Ware, cancer survivor

You were always one
to see the humour
in the most austere
situation:

the effects of chem-
otherapy grieved
others more – that shaved
crown! An amused gleam

of the eye measured
shock reactions,
never missed the chance
of making absurd

the hat your mother
lovingly knitted,
wore it at stupid
angles, brought laughter

from the pit. That the
accident outdoes
that sure wit stretches
credulity – I

imagine you in
shadow, awaiting
your moment to spring
out, merciful clown,

the frightful prank played.
But there's no respite,
Tim (the coffin shut,
the brief flowers laid

to rest.) Somehow I've
missed the joke. It's gone
far enough – come on
out! Scare me to life!

BEREAVEMENT

Life, they say, *goes on* –
omitting that people don't.

PIGEON FANCIER

He is one and wayward,
winding among
the loose skeins
of new-fallen leaves,
knows joy in the feel
of the moist grassed earth
underneath those soft child-soles.

We scatter crumbled bread,
he the pigeons
– reels to the uprush
of sight and sound
in that feathered blizzard.

Their blurs re-settle,
sidle round, peck:
he's in their midst
– spread arms, barrel-chested –
stumping about
with a sky-wide grin,
till the squall erupts again.

And we share the delight,
though at one step's remove;
smile in the knowledge
that, now he's found his feet,
he's in search of wings.

Blackmore Gardens, Sidmouth

EARTH

– and this piece in particular –
will serve my need for now.
We won't live here forever;
time's bound to move us on
in the end and eviction's
the only certainty.

But, for this evening,
this borrowed patch of ground
in this empire of thorn and weed
will nourish me
with its view of the hills,
that sense of somewhere else
above and beyond –
and the sunset
into which I'll someday ride.

Devon

AUTUMN STATEMENT

Less now on the trees,
though there's more on the ground
– all the Chancellor sees
is the fall
                    in the pound.

MIGRANT

One autumn
– with martins, swifts and swallows marshalling –
we waved you off
and settled to mundane concerns
under an English fall,
expecting you sometime the other side
of winter – in your eyes,
the dusty plains of India,
snows of Nepal.

Two autumns
and one near miss with cancer after that
first episode,
the season marked your gradient on
the rising paths of air.
We lost you in the mire of set routine
but looked to meet your gaze
fresh from the spiced and scented East,
your sojourn there.

This autumn
– as every autumn since your heart was claimed
elsewhere for good –
we watch migration-clouded skies
re-form, distantly blue
and empty; miss even your absences,
their forecast ends, and know
you won't come back to us – instead,
we'll follow you.

LOST BOY FOUND

Born this side of Eden,
start to lose my way,
ask the Lord to guide me,
now he here to stay.

Give me new direction,
turnin' me around,
say them holy angels singin'
lost boy found.

Meet this pretty lady,
sweetest in my life,
tell her really like it
if she be my wife.

When I know she love me,
feel like homeward bound,
all of my emotions shoutin'
lost boy found.

Wife she give me daughter,
wife she give me son,
then another boy
before the fam'ly done.

First time that I see them,
cry till nearly drowned,
joy to be their daddy 'cause I
lost boy found.

Sometime I get wayward,
know it a mistake,
sorry that it grieve the Lord
the mess I make.

Always there to comfort
when I hit the ground,
then he lift me up and say
lost boy found.

World it scar me badly,
make me wanna hide,
learn to keep the hurtin'
somewhere deep inside.

Parts of me long buried,
think they safe and sound
– Lord he dig them up and tell me
lost boy found.

Haven't finished trav'llin',
still got much to learn,
need help to be ready
for the Lord's return.

Hopin' to see heaven,
glory shine around,
wanna hear them angels sing
lost boy found.

THE RE-TUNING

I wasn't made
to go it alone
– whistling in the dark,
humming the broken tunes
of this fleeting exile.
I wasn't meant
to carry that burden.

In the Healing Presence,
the songs will mend;
in harmony with others,
I'll come to lift my voice
– distinct, though merging
into a greater whole –
and be part
of the music.

from

FOR THE SEASON: CHRISTMAS AND WINTER POEMS

A CHRISTMAS CACTUS

Abloom in mid-November,
this blushing herald flops
– redundant since September,
when upstaged in the shops.

ADVENT

We light candles
– another every week –
until the last kindles
and the four lights make

light for the Light.
World's Light.
True light.

For the Light-we-can't-hold-a candle-to-Light!

CAT AND THE SNOW

in memoriam Tilly, family cat 1978-1992

What can you see out there?
Dark room, dark panes, dark evening and the light
first fall of snow to listless earth
powders the paving.

Spellbound, your yellow eyes
focus beyond the glass. They are intent
on something else. Is it the night's
calm mystery?

Beneath that coarse, thick coat
– its motley insulating sound – there stirs
a fabled curiosity.
Gone from the sill,

will you investigate
that movement in the shrubbery, pursue
your moon-struck shadow's flight across
the snow-flecked lawn?

No further than the warm
dark of the kitchen: at the end you lie,
nursing the boiler-plate; like me,
wedded to comfort.

THE MOUSE AND HIS CHILD

after the novel by Russell Hoban

Clothed tin, the clockwork mice are wound,
father and son: they dance
their solemn circle, round and round
– fine-whiskered, glassy-eyed –
treading the counter, and entrance
the ragged man outside.

The father clasps the timid child,
swings him – first up, then down –
whirring until (with spring uncoiled)
he halts, his arms upraised
where his son faces the unknown:
the tramp stares back, amazed.

Turning, in mime, he moves his feet,
dances as they have done,
then lurches off; while, in the street,
a lost dog sniffs the snow
and follows where his prints lead on
the way the mice must go.

CHRISTMAS IS…

the time of year
when the rich think of the poor
and the poor think of the overdraft.

THE LESSON

Before they've learnt to read,
they're studying catalogues,
can decode the glossy images
with ease, delight.

Before they've learnt to write,
they're dictating Christmas lists,
letters to Santa Claus,
anticipating marvels.

Before they've learnt to count,
we start to estimate the cost
to their souls of the vain desires
that immoderate love has fed.

To a Service of Nine Lessons,
we append a tenth,
becoming cautionary
with *I want doesn't get!*
Or, to put things another way,
Thou shalt not covet.

ARRIVALS

for Kathryn and Matthew

Once – twice – I have stood
in those sterile rooms,
bewildered,
as your mother's arms
clenched, unclenched,
on the rigid bed;
as my tears drenched
her pillowed head
in the minute
that – birth-bruised, crumpled –
you floundered out
and changed my world.

And, alive
to each miracle,
I can believe
an unkempt stable
once witnessed
a greater far:
the girl's frame braced
to deliver
in the minute
that – birth-bruised, crumpled –
God floundered out
and changed our world.

Princess Margaret Hospital, Swindon

THE GIFT

One that I almost miss,
as I sift the mounds
of Christmas debris:
the festive layers
now wrenched aside,
the hollow packaging
that failed expectation.

And there's nothing here
that marks what I seek
with outward sign:
a gift quite unsurpassed,
save that it comes small
and wrapped in swaddling.

IMMANUEL

God with us.
With us God.
Us with God.

ACCORDING TO LOCALS

Rough lot, these shepherds, sloping in off the hills
of an evening: tipsy, excitable
– unruly, too, after a skinful.
Simpletons most, with some seasoned rascals
for good measure, every one a curse.
Doltish, they shamble across the district,
bring the place down. What else can you expect?
(professionally, they're all Sabbath-breakers!)
When you enquire, don't hope to get sense
of this bunch, lingering back behind the inn,
mooning and stupid. Rather save your breath
than invite their ludicrous assertions.
King in a stable! That's the thing I mean:
next they'll be saying God's from Nazareth!

ERRATA (CHRISTMAS MEDLEY)

God rest you merry gentlemen,
let not this you dismay:
the chances are our Saviour
was born some other day
than this one which perpetuates
tradition gone astray,
    though tidings of comfort and joy,
        comfort and joy,
    though tidings of comfort and joy.

Not with heavy drifts of snow
was His birth announced below;
chroniclers, so it appears,
missed the proper date by years.
    Hail the Saviour, not the morn,
    and – when all its wraps lie torn –
    sing through every season then:
    Christ is born and Christ knows when!

What if the poets
got it wrong?
Maybe I'm a pedant,
yet I sing along;
while, among the homeless,
Christ survives
in the bleak midwinter
of our lives.

A WINTER WALK

for Christine

Towards noon, half the day
disposed to lethargy,
we ventured forth to see
the old year on its way

in mildly smarting air.
Its currents took us where
concrete blocks looming near
receded, skies swept clear

uncluttered the horizon.
Gentled, a winter sun
warmed us as we strolled on
in hopeful light far down

the shorn lanes, while the winds
unstrung the indoor mind's
cobwebs – long, bearded strands
teased lightly from the hands.

Pyrford, Surrey

“SHOULD AULD ACQUAINTANCE...”

Midnight. The echoing chime
as glass sounds off glass
on the champagne-buoyant air
of the party...

                    Round the globe,
time’s latest frontier
dissolves, crumbles away
in hours, to realign
twelve months up the shadowy road
no-one has trod before.

And, in the space that divides
the making and the breaking
of a thousand resolutions,
the armies massed on the borders
cross and the refugees
cross and their ravaged homesteads
ignite the darkness behind.

Here it’s *Auld Lang Syne*,
there more like *déjà vu*,
and the only cup is a bitter
ferment of violence.

And there’s no difference between
this and the ousted year:
it’s wine, warmth, music, mirth,
to some; to others slow
agonies in the cold
within earshot of the guns
fraying the gauze of sleep.
They’ll cross our screens tomorrow
but not our minds tonight,

since we make the usual toast.
Drink, then – to drown their sorrow.

THE ADORATION OF THE MAGI

Did they leave kingdoms
to negotiate desert,
subject themselves
to some higher law?

Did they leave families
beneath the eastern sky,
their love-lit features
forsaken for the star?

And the gifts – had they plenty
to spare in the vaults?
Or was each one prized,
rare stuff of sacrifice?

Had they commitments, duties
not lightly laid to one side?
Did their going come
as a burden to others?

I sift the account,
but the answers aren't given
and winds have long displaced
those tracks across the sand.

They have left no hint
that they found less reason than I
to excuse themselves
from this costly worship.

TWELFTH NIGHT

A wistful observance:
the images spooled back
and back, till the first frame
gives us the last.

We wake, now,
from that effortless trance,
the coiled sweetness
of its midwinter dream,

to a wasted hearth:
the treeless living room
dismal, prosaic
with undecoration.

And we gaze with eyes
abandoning their mirth
on the night's misrule,
its inverted magic:

all's sombre, workaday,
and the fortnight's leave
has to be avenged
in an unhealed world

with its irksome questions…
Is the debt very high?
How long before the spring?
And are we changed?

THE CHRISTMAS TREE

In the nearly-night
of a winter's afternoon,
we made our choice
among the nursery pines
humbled for the season:
you were swaddled, enmeshed,
trawled the long road home.

In the fairy-light
of the festive living room
– dressed like the earth's green king –
we welcomed you,
placing the customary tributes
over the heaving boughs
circling your young stem.

In the barely-light
of the new year's early gloom,
we stood you out
to face the elements
and cursed the needles in our carpets,
enduring unwillingly
their pointed sermon.

IDENTIFICATIONS

The Magi in Herod's palace before the king:
unwitting spies and informants.

Herod briefing his lieutenants:
a strong ruler protecting the national interest.

The soldiers killing the innocents:
good men obeying orders to keep *their* children alive.

The Holy Family leaving Bethlehem by night:
Jews fleeing the Holocaust.

AFTER EPIPHANY

So what of the Child?

Others, now, make the return:
shepherds to sheep,
wise men to counsel
and we – like the star – to more usual courses.

Where will *He* go?

Is He forever destined
to be born, adored, wrapped
and once more consigned
to the mind's attic
– a back-in-a-box redeemer
disrupting fixed routine
to emerge, a twelve-day wonder,
once in each twelve-month year?

We miss – not the Presence
(that itself seemed removed
from the excess that beset the celebration);
more the sense of its imminence
in the glimmer of stars,
in the carolling dark,
in the night frost's expectancy.

That's all behind
and the earth turns back
and away towards summer,
though it's six months off
and the most unholy cold
is still to come.

Yet, if you choose to look,
the Child is to be found:
between His parents on the southern roads,

headed for exile and the obscurity
of the mission station or transit camp;
skirting the enclaves of the dispossessed,
their fearful no man's land.

He waits – silent, among the destitute –
to meet your gaze, awaken your compassion.

WHEN WILL WE HEAR YOU SING THAT SONG AGAIN?

It came once to others,
shook the hill-dark
that circled Bethlehem,
and tumbled shepherds
in alleyways,
whirled like the snows
in a child's transparent dome.

We've caught echoes,
strains on the midnight air
worlds, centuries, distant;
in carols sensed
that purer, higher theme
soaring aloft
– an exquisite descant.

But the sound we hear
is momentary, lost
before the ear gets it whole:
nothing to touch
that first performance
or stir the heart
like the original.

Though it's said you keep watch
over us still
– invisible guardians –
we doubt the substance
of unattested claims,
wild-eyed assertions made
of your immanence.

And yet we long
for the skies to part,
filling the emptiness
around and within
with your ancient song,
winging “Peace on earth”
to all – yes, even us.

MOTHER OF GOD

So Mary treasured it all up
and wondered at these signs that moved
scholars and countrymen to stoop
in homage to her heart's beloved.

And wondered more – seeing the lad
join in the ordinary play
of neighbours' boys, fall, hurt his head,
then let her dab his tears away
– that it was God she comforted.

from

THE HEDGEHOG HOUSE: POEMS OF SPRING AND EASTER

FEBRUARY EVENING

There's snow
and the first daffs
tilt their nodding lamps
to the coming dusk.

THE SPRING COLLECTION

It's still winter
and, in the High Street,
The Spring Collection
is the only sign
that the earth's on the mend.

Our pale reflections
slide across store windows:
mannequins loll behind,
party to the event
– out here, it's on ice.

And we long to shed
these besmirched and weathered layers
for the cool attire that greets
those balmy days
the shops anticipate.

By the time spring comes,
they'll be awash with swimsuits;
then, *Back To School*
will cloud the summer gaze
of youth in the long vacation.

On into autumn,
the fashions reel,
their cut and colour
outstripping the doomed leaves:
we dance to their figure.

Through three months' worth
of Christmas velvets,
we waltz, arriving once more
at these fresh designs,
their in-store renaissance

– the new variation
on an insistent theme:
that, to keep in step,
we accelerate change,
wish ourselves on a season.

Year after year,
it's the same old pattern
that vies with impermanence –
styles currently in vogue
merge with yesterday's.

And – once in the cycle –
dead hopes revive,
stirring towards spring
when April spreads rumours
from the mouth of the tomb:

promises whispered
of a snow-white garment
and the body to match
– one made to last
from here to eternity.

THAW

Even down here,
in the Gulf Stream's mild embrace,
there's snow sometimes
at the end of the winter –

scarcely enough to arrest
the change of season,
another year's growth; yet we know
some things don't ever make it,

hardly begin to stir
in the vast womb of the earth
before they're shed
with its meltwater.

Unmourned, unacknowledged,
their cells disperse,
forgotten beneath
the surface profusion.

It's as if spring miscarried
in the early weeks
only to bear again,
unmindful of her dead.

But thaw unlocks
the cataracts of grief,
fresh buds call into the mind
others the world won't see.

I think of these
as I walk, silent,
among the ragged heads
of storm-bruised crocuses.

I think of severed roots,
promise the late frost blights.
I think of joys denied
and I think of you.

Devon

DIARY ENTRY

Not the kind of day
to be much remembered,
it was marked for me only
– walking its grey lanes –
by the vague shapes of trees
marooned in mist and river-marsh:
great trunks of willow, gnarled and twisted,
like the overturned ghosts
of a wreck, their lank hair
trailed on the slow tide of damp air.

North Hinksey, Oxford

IN TRANSIT

I had thought spring
more immediate
in its healing
– the earth's flesh
rinsed and revived,
stirring to April warmth.

Instead, just this murmur,
this gentling of winds –
its quiet interval
an arm up
in the struggle
to get clear of winter.

And we've some way yet!
It's a stiff climb, still,
to the May woods
– light-filtered, bluebell-clustered -
cresting the downs.
Weeks off, we know

that spring is the ache
in tired limbs,
the feverish pulse
that jars in the brain,
as we strain towards
unimagined wholeness.

DIVINE SERVICE

on Maundy Thursday

Twenty-four feet –
road-reeking, foul.
Two hands deployed
with a basin and towel.

FOREIGN EXCHANGE

Not many steps
between here and Golgotha,
yet it's worlds away
beneath this staggering load.

Blood drips, blurs the vision,
and I stumble
– my curt guards
seize on the African.

Simon, I want your arms
to bear these huge timbers,
lift them towards
their rightful destination.

Our eyes meet
as you're hauled from the crowd,
still clutching at
the morning's schedule.

Lay down that burden
and shoulder mine.
Then, I'll carry yours
– until it's gone for ever!

GOOD FRIDAY PROCESSION

Rain – soft yet persistent –
pelts the subdued crowd,
stipples the scene
with its quiet anguish,

making of these back roads
(familiar to the eye
since the first parades
of that lost boyhood)

a Way of Tears,
an interstice of pain
between houses, gardens,
small stores and offices.

And the cross trawls
their meandering length,
raising the gathered guilts
of the neighbourhood

on its splayed, unwieldy
gantry arms.
I move in its wake
as the soft rain quickens,

aiming a gentle scourge
across senses, soul,
at the inmost self
– mute, withdrawn, yet accepting

the sky's reproach
for the undeserved,
the protracted death,
which my silence allowed.

Byfleet, Surrey

"MOTHER, THIS IS YOUR SON"

It's an unjust world:
I saw you enter,
I've seen you go;
and there's nothing more to be done,
except for the burial
(that much too hasty – the Sabbath's coming!)
with all the days remaining
to mourn an eldest son
cut off near the height of his powers.

It was your arm
that I caught at when Joseph died,
that upheld me in widowhood
with young mouths to feed.
The family business
thrived at your hands
– timber crafted, stone
shaped with more expertise
even than Joseph's.

If you'd only stayed,
maintained that godly silence
and shown in your work
how we all should live!
Yet it wasn't enough
and you started down the road
that pitched you up
on this desolate hill
reserved for the vagabond, thief,
misguided and arrogant.

Classed among such
in the minds of the pragmatists,
I witness your demise
– the son I used to know.
John's here beside me

as your body's lowered, now,
waymarked with suffering:
whipped, crucified, speared – all this
and you still manage
to lend me an arm!

THOMAS AND THE LORD

Thomas
saw scars,
touched belief,
cured doubt.

The Lord
saw belief,
touched doubt,
cured scars.

GARAGE FLOWERS

Too many gifts
end up as garage flowers,
like the daffodil bulbs
left there in autumn,
until there's more time
for planting, nurture.

In spring you enter,
to root for garden tools,
and the carrier's burst
– the green stalks rise,
pale heads reflecting
something they always sensed.

And you know they need
the soil of the earth.
You know *we* need
their fragile, though spirited, blooms.
They've lived too long
in the joyless dark:
reach for the trowel
– bring them to light!

NATURAL JAZZ

Across the road
they're a tightly-formed group
at the edge of the lawn
– daffs, bright and brassy,
hunching in
at the nape to produce
their echoes of sun
in the bells of those golden horns.

There's a wind on the hill:
they dance, cavort,
alive with a sense
of summer coming
(though they'll have gone),
swaying in time
to their colourful music
– keep them in sight
and you'll almost catch the sound.

THE HEDGEHOG HOUSE

I have dismantled the hedgehog house.
It stood all winter, its gaunt cage
bristling at the edge of the garden
under spent apple trees – that spiny mound
of twigs and branches pruned two summers back.

Ditched first behind the garage and then moved
within view of the house in a tidy fit
(they never last!), it scuffed the ragged lawn,
discarded limbs meshed in the random pose
that a child's keen eyes interpreted.

In the instant she gave voice to it,
I understood the name, what it implied:
how the sticks mounted in effigy
the hunched profile of the said incumbent
whose winter quarters it was deemed to be.

The long rains filtered down. The grass grew up
over it, until the hovel reared
barrow-like across at us. We imagined
the creature buried there, invulnerable
as some Iron Age chieftain on the downs.

Yet when, in spring, the structure was unroofed
– the lifeless debris bagged and tossed aside –
its chamber yielded nothing to show
the prickly fellow had been there at all
or used it at one time and arisen.

Whether or not he hibernated there,
the hedgehog is abroad and clambering
among the earth's freedoms lustily;
it matters little where he left his bed,
that this rough bivouac proved obsolete.

I have dismantled the hedgehog house.
Its tense prison had outfaced the need,
but no more than other misplaced things
I've kept around me, still to be dismantled,
pending this season of vacated tombs.

AT ASCENSION

We're used to gravity,
the harsh insistence
of the inevitable earth;
to high hopes,
let-downs,
bravery
and bruises.

We're used to sin,
the rash persuasions
of the easy flesh;
to good intentions,
ill-effects,
ideals
and excuses.

We're unaccustomed
to smooth ascents,
to defying the odds
in either department.
But this Day confounds
with its staggering reversal,
heaven's buoyant logic:
what comes down
must go up.

PERSONAL EFFECTS

In memory of Tim Ware, 1964-1992

... 'You're a hopeless romantic,' said Faber. 'It would be funny if it were not serious. It's not books you need, it's some of the things that once were in books... No, no, it's not books at all you're looking for! Take it where you can find it, in old phonograph records, old motion pictures, and in old friends; look for it in nature and look for it in yourself. Books were only one type of receptacle where we stored a lot of things we were afraid we might forget.'

... Granger stood looking back with Montag. 'Everyone must leave something behind when he dies, my grandfather said. A child or a book or a painting or a house or a wall or a pair of shoes made. Or a garden planted. Something your hand touched some way so your soul has somewhere to go when you die, and when people look at that tree or that flower you planted, you're there.'

RAY BRADBURY: FAHRENHEIT 451

They are everything the soul
relinquished for death
– the most immediate,
those found near or at
the scene of the accident, crime
or simply inevitable:
Clothes worn at the time;
cheque book, pen, wallet, key
to assorted mysteries – with,
perhaps, the fob? Disused body.

*

That last
makes nonsense of the rest,
robs them of meaning, lets
them fall

– like those bright, circling inanimates,
if the juggler's hands fumble.

*

Later, there are the rooms
to be faced, to clear
or maybe leave – museums
of absence, emptier
for their lifeless totems
standing in unbreathed air.

*

Strange that my brother's
avoids either extreme,
domiciles visitors
without negating him
– his furtive presence
beneath the sloping roof

that I slept under, once
(it was my last remove
procured him the key!)
My children sleep there, now,
on visits to grandparents – and comfortably –
yet it's *his* room somehow.

*

It's the books
that intrigue me most.
The shelves maintain the silence of their load:
the *Lonely Planet* guides, the Kerouacs
we never discussed
– *Lonesome Traveller* and *On the Road*.

Two amateur critics,
we almost crossed
on the highways they construed.

*

And the records.
They're played often enough,
some of them: the sounds and words
he listened – moved – to, once.

Return the needle, let the song revive,
but his feet no longer dance.

*

I scan the lyrics,
hoping to descry
between the line-breaks
his philosophy:

one that gives meaning
to his life, his death,
this side of breathing
– a viable faith.

Though I've tried The Doors
and The Waterboys,
neither delivers
the authentic voice

that's gone forever,
but the last tells me
that was the river
and *this is the sea*.

*

There's more of sense
in the diaries
– the incisive journals
kept upon travels
in the Far East, the Antipodes:

weathered leaves mapped
with accounts, observations
the mind's camera snapped;
musings on poverty;
worlds interpreted
with wit, irony
and unfeigned compassion
– qualities known
almost better dead.

*

I have – for posterity –
the harmonica,
perhaps, that served as company,
deep in the bush that night,
for the lone backpacker
beneath Mount Freycinet.

Re-reading the entry
moves me, still – and yet
no more could I say why,
although I experiment,
than articulate
the unlearned instrument.

*

He wore my cast-offs
during his youth
– stigmata of a second son.
Among my griefs,
I count the truth
that my best suit's this hand-me-down,
broad around the shoulders
– in death it would appear
the living roles reverse:
he's become the elder.

*

They are, at best, clues
and clues only
– these objects which survive,
years on, the loss –
to the unsolved mystery
not of the death but the life.

*

But the family home
is eventually sold on;
no longer will its walls
afford us such welcome.

So we apportion
everything we've held
within its confines – spoils
of the life that chance dismantled.

Needful diaspora!
We manage it somehow,
re-distribute the hoard
– grief's memorabilia –

knowing it has to go:
all that once was his,
now more widely scattered
than the body's ashes.

*

Catalogue it all:
make an inventory
and omit no detail
from the history
– were we now to recall
the entirety,
we might not reassemble
that once-known entity.

*

Effects we call them,
lifeless mementoes
of the dead life we will always mourn:
their prime focus

to keep alive the name
this side of a bodily resurrection.

But, though all were lost
beyond recovery,
like the deceased,
his influence would sustain
itself in memory
– one enduring strand
woven into the skein
of the lives left behind.

DISMANTLING NO MAN'S LAND

To Chris, with whom I share this no man's land

A VIEW OF THE TIP

Behind the rank allotments, cars piled up
with debris pause: the usual Sunday queues,
swaying beneath their burdens, mount the slope
and from the platform's edge discharge their refuse.

Passing, we shake our heads, sigh and declaim
using the Sabbath thus as a forsworn thing,
but check such thoughts, having done much the same,
who shed their load in church only this morning.

Swindon, Wiltshire

AT ABINGER HAMMER

Bringing the children when I got the chance
– once in a summer, maybe, on a stay
with parents turned grandparents, sisters aunts –
I'd make the journey back for this half-day

remembering by the milling Tilling Bourne…
Nothing much altered on arrival: there's
the clock, the smith, working in unison;
the green, at weekends sporting cricketers.

We leave the car, stroll to the bus shelter
and watch across the street its artisan
striking the bell. Those chimes – one! two! three! four! –
recall teas bolted as the next hour ran

to meet us seated once more opposite,
eyes on the hand poised there to hammer five,
both parents with us on a Sunday treat:
my sisters, I, the brother then alive.

Some things confound the urge to reconstruct:
back down the road from Gomshall, on the bend
– the entrance antique-stuffed – Grimm's Kitchen's
locked.
No longer do the hikers now descend

to place their orders: tea and sandwiches
(served on clean china) generously spread
then crammed with leafy mounds of watercress,
harsh-flavoured produce of the riverbed.

There's bitterness also in some events
which separate that time and who I am
today – one casualty's the innocence,
another this self-same Elysium

marred, now, by tragedy. It is as though
masonry off an old waterside house,
dislodging, hit the runnel down below
and smashed the image in its moving glass.

Close by, the children tramp over the bridge
and, shedding shoes and clothes, wade in the stream;
watching above them on the bank's turfed edge,
I gaze with wonder at the happy dream

they've reawakened. This may never be
for them the touchstone of experience
that, since my youth, it has become to me
– the place of wholeness, where it all makes sense –

and yet, in other settings, they'll divine,
nearer to home perhaps, the tranquil joy
that lives in memories akin to mine
of timeless moments shared: the harmony

between these human dwellings, this expanse
of grass and trees (the North Downs' ridge behind)
and the Bourne running through its sunlit trance
– I hold the vision, map it in the mind.

THE NEWBORN BREAKFAST EARLY

Your mother's shape in the huddled bedclothes:
the before-dawn landscape.

Your cry upon waking:
a slow kettle starting to boil.

WHERE YOU ARE

for Jonathan James, b. May 16th, 1995 – d. May 28th, 1995

Where you are,
the lungs renew themselves
perpetually.

Where you are,
the atmosphere is mild enough
for the most delicate skin.

Where you are,
the heart is sound
and the guarantee eternal.

Where you are,
the food's good and the service excellent
all the time.

Where you are,
spinsters are embraced
and childless uncles
make entertainments for the unborn.

Where you are,
tears are obsolete
and the currency of pain
has been permanently withdrawn.

Where you are,
the sad are comforted,
the homeless housed,
the hungry fed,
the sick made whole

and the only hands with scars
are the Surgeon’s.

GEOGRAPHY

to Matthew, aged four

“Where’s heaven, Daddy?” What am I to say,
when neither time nor distance renders proof?
You ask, “Is it a long, long far away?”

I will not have it in the sky above,
given that rockets pierce the atmosphere
without arriving at that last remove.

“Heaven’s where God is.” “God is everywhere.”
My words come back at me – *where God is*, so
their logic moves, *God’s everywhere. God’s here.*

Here’s heaven. In a sense, maybe, although
imperfectly – there’s much that doesn’t fit
the definition. Worse, sometimes I know

experience suggests the opposite.
Which notwithstanding, how do I explain
that heaven’s where all things are made complete?

The happiness that, here, is edged with pain;
dreams life may never fully realize;
healing begun, albeit scars remain;

the holy in terrestrial enterprise
– all culminate in its untainted air,
invested with a wholeness I surmise

our present joys dimly to harbinger,
their measure infinitely magnified.
A long, long far away? Yes, and more near

than this fond heart now beating at your side.

FIRST NAME

to Kathryn

Yesterday, in school,
someone called you a "bitch"
for no justifiable reason.
Back home, it was with speech
we sought to draw the poison,
who named you "Pure" when small.

We'd ward off every dart
yet know still more will come
so arm you well enough
to combat their venom,
emblazoning with love
this shield around your heart.

Though the world slander you,
daughter, hurl nothing back
to reinforce the lie;
in countering its attack,
bear the more gallantly
that first name – the most true.

PARENT PSALM

I wake early
and go to bed late.

Between times, there are the children
to dress, feed, help prepare
for the day's events
(an unwieldy timetable
of classes and clubs,
most miles apart
and all in close succession);
their bread and mine to earn
in the marketplace;
and the house to keep
in some semblance of order…

Where's God in all this?
Unanswerable question,
it scrolls with me
around the treadmill of the day.
I stumble to its end
– the routine now reversed
for that final tilt,
headlong towards bed
and oblivion –
clinging on to the sense
that all my ways are known.

HOMECOMING

A coffin draped
in the Royal Standard
is airlifted
across the Channel
to an island gripped
with grief's inertia.

The plane lands,
furrowing English soil:
the fairy tale ends
and the summer's over.

31st August, 1997

*

And so the stations
of national mourning:
the sojourning
at the palaces
– regal St James's, Kensington's –
and the thousands
of tense, expectant faces
lining the route
to the Abbey;
the jingling horse-drawn gun-carriage;
the prayers, the oratory
and the silent tribute.

Then, the cortege
moving off and away,
winding down city streets
and on up country

to Althorp's gates;
and – beyond – the sanctuary
of an island within an island,
where once the girl found peace
who now returns, Princess,
for ever to this home ground.

1st – 6th September, 1997

*

Dawn breaks.
And the heart.
Rain swells the sombre air
as England awakes
to the smart
of no Diana.

7th September, 1997

PASSENGERS

Boarding life's train before their destinations
have been announced, most travel hopefully,
though some will disembark between the stations,
thinking that stop affords more certainty.

ONE OF THESE DAYS, PERHAPS

to Christine

One of these days, perhaps,
we'll get the house in order
and everything will keep
its station; you and I
will sit, of an evening,
free from the irksome thought
of all we've left not done
– perhaps, one of these days.

One of these days, perhaps,
we'll have the garden tidy:
the lawn mown, edges clipped
and trees and bushes pruned
of their excess; we'll stroll the paths,
not hampered with a sense
of encroaching wilderness
– perhaps, one of these days…

Yet, if we never live
to see it come around,
we'll hold that end in mind,
strive to attain its view.
One of these days, perhaps,
this heart will understand
that it was enough to know
I shared the mess with you.

DAVY DANCES

Davy dances:
with a bound,
he's in his place,
sways to the sound

of – it could be –
the stereo,
telly
or the radio;

bends the knees
and bobs around,
bum just inches
off the ground.

Davy dances:
themes of soaps,
commercial space,
Top of the Pops;

hears the first bar,
hits the floor,
eager
self-choreographer

of cheerful classics
(minus socks)
with earthquakes
when he rolls and rocks!

Davy dances:
let him dance,
embrace
with such extravagance

all the joy
that Heaven bestows,
soul and body
– head, heart, *toes*.

Let him,
in the dance, endorse
the rhythm
of the universe.

FATHER TO THE MAN

The most amazing truth of parenthood:
that how I think of you, God thinks of me.

*

It overwhelms, this magnitude of trust:
you sleep and wake untroubled in my arms.

*

Joys re-discovered, these shared interests:
books and tales, football, jigsaw puzzles, trains.

*

I've given much less than I have received:
loving you, I have learned to love myself.

*

The greatest compliment a son could give:
"When I grow up I want to be a dad."

IN DODD'S LANE

To turn left, disappear between
the roadside dwellings here, is to
venture once more upon the uncertain
ground that my adolescence knew.

The lane, the houses, peter out;
the path bisects the field beyond;
thereafter, everything's in doubt,
sprawling through uneven woodland.

Ahead, the bridge (and smooth canal
dappled with light): ragged hedgerows
nourish old griefs and the earth still
carries the imprint of my woes.

Headlong, I'd stumble to attain
the far bank, the more level ways
of ambling towpath, pulsing vein
of water – calm and effortless

after the fearful lane. My sons
will, no doubt, travel some such road,
harried like me the fraught distance
between childhood and adulthood.

What gift in me will help them, then,
except the memory of this – so
anguished – trajectory of pain?
Only this hushed "I know. I know."

Pyrford, Surrey

MILLENNIUM LETTER

Dear Tim, eight years have gone since we last met.
It was after Christmas; you were home
from Bexhill and we came over that day
to exchange gifts and see everyone
– observe the season. Matthew was a mere
ten or eleven weeks and you held him
for the second time – he still talks about you,
although I can't imagine he'd remember
that one embrace in all the multitudes
in infancy.

Within a month we'd moved
to Devon. You were amongst the first to 'phone
– that same weekend – wish us well in the new house.
You said you hoped to make the journey down
to visit in the summer and the thought
reduced the entire South Coast to a single bay
with you at one end and me at the other.

You left me, then, to unpack. I'd love to call you,
describe what's happened in the interim:
how Matthew's grown, loves football, enjoys school
and muses on the maps in atlases
of an evening; Kathryn, eleven, still
goes to bed hugging Pluto – the plush toy Disney
character you once gave her – plans to own
a whole menagerie when older, with,
among other things, a capybara
to keep the grass in check! You won't know
their little brother David – his intense,
volatile moods: one minute charm itself,
the next totally at odds with everyone
and everything – a true child of extremes.
An expert on steam engines!

Chris and I?
We're happy, if hard-pressed to reconcile
the unremitting schedules of employment
with parenthood's demands. Between the two,
there's little leisure for the finer things.
Or money, come to that! New Year saw in
the Third Millennium: with all the hype
before the event, you could be forgiven
for thinking it some kind of watershed
in human history, yet it seems to me
that life's really no different – except you
aren't in it or part of it any more.

We keep your photo on the piano:
you're standing in the cable-car; behind,
the mountains circle – wry, amused, you gaze
from the centre of the picture, that half-grin
disarming with its sense almost of one
who's looked death calmly in the eye and knows
that it means nothing once the dying's done.

CONSTANT

A child dies
in hospital,
wired up to instruments
that manufacture breath.
His parents watch
as the doctors "let him go"
– only their love
holds him in the end.

A child dies
in the open air;
the unchecked cholera
wastes his putrid flesh.
His parents watch,
helpless to stem its tide
– only their love
holds him to the end.

Between two hemispheres,
love's the equator:
the one constant
among variables
like the standard of medical care
and the price of sparrows.

UNTITLED

Your coming more ill-timed
than unwelcome, they sought advice
and took “the most sensible option”;
you were consigned, unknown,
to anonymity.

Years on, they still wonder:
Were you a boy? A girl?
And with what unique traits
suppressed? Of one thing they’re sure:
in different circumstances,
you would have been adored.

And everything since then
seems more equivocal,
more chance than otherwise,
an erring off the path
that looked towards life with you.

Always, the thought pervades
their minds: *If you were here…*
Yet *all* would have to change
before that rupture healed.
You are the road not taken,
the happy freight derailed.

ON DEMAND

It's a matter of conscience
and conscience must guide:
the individual
will have to decide.

They say that life's sacred;
the trouble begins
when you clarify terms
– it depends what *life* means.

Is it something that happens
when atoms converge
or always in doubt
till it's seen to emerge?

It's a question of values:
we're given the choice,
but the one most affected
is left with no voice

– ignored, disenfranchised,
condemned without plea
to this privatisation
of morality.

THE ENGLAND OF A. R. QUINTON

A quintessential rural scene
on the postcard: we easily imagine
the bicycle against the hedge
beyond the watercolour's edge

as, with his pencil, he records
the rambling lanes, the trickling fords,
the comely greens, the homely press
of thatch on wayside cottages

beneath a tranquil sky – its hue
worked up in the studio
months later (foil to amber gold
in open copse, on sunlit wold)

with country men and women set
about the village and estate
or, on the road since roads began,
the archetypal travelling man.

Enchanted, we absorb the view,
know the delight the artist knew,
then saunter off with maps unfurled
to rediscover Quinton's world

– a world now vanished, we surmise
yet in his landscapes visualize
the England of a yesterday
only a bicycle away.

EDWARD THOMAS MEETS HIS MAKER

I never quite understood what was meant by God.
EDWARD THOMAS, WAR DIARY

As if you – as if anyone – could
know the Unknowable! It's in that "quite",
I sense your approach to the Mystery:
wry, questioning, uneasy of exact
formalism, like the starched Sunday clothes
which stifled one whole day in every seven
infancy's wild delights. The "country creed"
you handed down was a more generous fit,
divining in the nearness of the earth
– its unruffled acceptance of your moods –
eternity, familiar to the touch.

And yet, elsewhere, you described missing chapel
at Oxford as being tantamount to "the lack
of a mother's sweetness" in one's nursery years:
nothing the future held would compensate
that fundamental deprivation.
Thereafter, notions of the Infinite
were unemphatic, if speculative
– moved to affirm "There's nothing like the sun",
you'd add the codicil, "till we are dead."

So – on the morning that a missile strayed
across Beaurains, dismantling No Man's Land
(you with it) and your soul rose disattired –
was it to face heaven's righteous pedantry
or meet someone whose works you'd long admired?

IN DEPENDENCE

You're woven into childhood
with all that soppy stuff
and, if doubt frays the garment,
we can't quite shake you off.

We outgrow pixies, fairies,
gnomes and elves (all that crew
deployed round Santa's workshop),
yet still cling on to you

– more as insurance cover
(you are life's big Perhaps)
or simply an expletive
to use when things collapse.

But always in the background
– like an unhealing scar –
your name throbs, posing questions:
who, what and *if* you are?

Some say that you're within us,
some that you're way out there;
some think you love us deeply,
some wonder if you care;

some assume you went missing
once the earth was in place,
some think you're all that stops us
veering off into space;

some insist you're a Person,
some more a cosmic Force;
some "demonstrate" your power,
others dispute the source.

Mostly, your shape eludes us.
We probe the Mystery:
your arms stretch on the crossbar
that makes the I a T.

There – twenty centuries distant –
you wrestle human doubts.
Experts square up, contesting
your present whereabouts.

Angels said you were living.
Nietsche pronounced you dead.
Who else is there to clothe us?
Give us our daily bread.

ANGELUS

...Christ in you, the hope of glory.
COLOSSIANS 1:27

1. MORNING

Flesh.
This human flesh.
Halting frame that scatters
– on objects, surfaces –
its mark of origin.

Exposed when sunlight enters.
Caught on the still beam.
Motes in sunlight, dancing;
dust over mantelpiece, sill,
shelves and ornaments.

I give you mine.
This human flesh.
Dust on the scales.
Scales of dust.
It's all I have.
It's all I am.
This flesh.

2. NOON

Word.
Incarnate Word.
Mind that raised flesh from dust,
raised dust to life.

Knowing the day's fierce heat.
Toiling beneath the sun.
The brow at midday, sweating;
weariness in the arms,
emptying finite flesh.

Flesh like mine.
This human flesh.
Veiling God's Word.
His Living Word.
That made the world.
Entered the world.
Became flesh.
Human flesh.

3. NIGHT

Christ.
Indwelling Christ.
God in this human frame.
His Word embodied
in halting flesh
that scatters dust,
veiling the Origin.

Piercing the heavy darkness.
Lighting the sombre room.
The dust, the flesh, transfigured;
the holy, humanised
in Christ the Infinite.

Inhabit mine.
This human flesh.
Be all I have.
Be all I am.
This flesh.

Notes on *Subdued Anthems*

Subdued Anthems combines material originally circulated between 2002 and 2010 via the Hedgehog House imprint. The five pamphlets released during that period have been revised for this back catalogue volume and some material that I am uncomfortable with at this distance removed. Decisions regarding the exclusion or otherwise of poems were generally around questions of adequacy, although – at times – emotional significance was of more importance with me than technical merit. On this basis, the contents of *The Songs of Exile*, *Personal Effects* and *Dismantling No Man's Land* have not been altered and are offered "warts and all". Both *For the Season* and *The Hedgehog House* included compositions that I'd say, with hindsight, were permitted originally to make up the numbers. For this collection, ten of these poems have therefore been removed. Those left, however idiosyncratic, continue to affect me in some measure and therefore keep their position. The notes that follow give some context to the individual collections.

The Songs of Exile

Conceptually, *The Songs of Exile* was around before any of my other collections of poetry with much of its content generated in the Nineties (not the most comfortable decade in my life, though one with very genuine compensations.) Given this, the theme of exile – and, indeed, some of the poems themselves – originated even further back. At one stage in its development, the collection embraced more than forty poems. However, it was eventually cut to twenty-six in view of my uneasiness with some of these, among them several of the most ambitious efforts. It was never their intention that troubled me – only their inadequacy – and any idea of publication was delayed to allow time for revision. By about 2005, it was apparent to me that, despite these absences, the remaining poems had begun to cohere into something approaching wholeness and that the others – if ever completed – might ultimately sit elsewhere. If the collection centres on various exiles or separations and the loss that attends them, it is also concerned (I hope it is, anyway) with how we live with and beyond them, finding joy in the midst of imperfection.

For the Season

Other than the earlier *Cat and the Snow* and *The Mouse and His Child*, all of these poems have their origins in the Nineties. They came about individually and it was some time before the idea of the seasonal theme developed. Interestingly, though, I've traced the notion back to 1985. Honeymooning near Dolgellau, Wales, my wife Chris and I discovered the town bookshop. Among the purchases we made was George Mackay Brown's *Christmas Poems*. Years later, this small collection with its wood-cut illustrations – though very different in style and tone – inspired the cover design for the 2002 edition of the pamphlet *For the Season*. Wood-cuts weren't an option, so computer images manipulated then overlaid with corrugated triangles of thin card under one smudge of gold ink suggested the opening of *The Christmas Tree*.

Since childhood, I've approached Christmas with visionary expectation. Year after year – despite the madness, the materialism – I've hoped for that deep realisation, that inner sense, that somehow God's with us. Invariably, I'm disappointed. Perhaps, though, I'm mistaken in thinking there's some equivalent for the soul of the Christmas dinner, the surfeit that most of us in Western society experience. That's one more indulgence and it seems to me, now, that – if anywhere – Christ's encountered in others, that, if Christmas amounts to anything more than an attempt to insulate against the cold and the dark, it's in the value that it attributes to human beings, particularly the vulnerable.

It is important to emphasise that, although *Arrivals* is dedicated to Kathryn and Matthew, it was completed several years prior to the equally significant appearance – at quite another maternity unit – of their brother David.

The Hedgehog House

I suppose it was logical that, if my Christmas and winter poems were organised thematically, the spring and Easter ones might also merit this treatment. They got it, anyway, and *The Hedgehog House* resulted. *Diary Entry* dates back to the Eighties, although virtually everything else included here belongs to the next decade except for *Divine Service* commissioned in the new millennium. It's my guess that, even with some excisions, the poems vary in quality and that, in some instances, they'd be different if attempted again. Among them, even so, I've identified several that I consider to be among my very best compositions – *Good Friday Procession*, *The Hedgehog House*, perhaps *February Evening*.

Personal Effects

At the age of only twenty-seven – on the afternoon of April 20th, 1992 – my younger brother Tim died when his vehicle collided with another on the A21 near Tunbridge Wells. It was Easter Monday. Ironically, he had recently beaten testicular cancer and was looking forward to re-building his life following this scare. Much of my grief was voiced in *The Songs of Exile*, although the bereavement also informs *Dismantling No Man's Land* with its increased sense of vulnerability. In the mix at about the same time, *Personal Effects* – with its somewhat irregular and experimental form – records the journey between *Coming to Terms* and *Millennium Letter*. Despite its emotional significance, I'm uncertain of the sequence's technical merit and offer it on this understanding, knowing only that it was helpful to me in adjusting to Tim's death without necessarily making wonderful poetry.

Dismantling No Man's Land

The story of this collection is – with some overlap – the sequel to *The Songs of Exile*. Developmentally, its content extends from the Eighties (*A View of the Tip*) into the early years of the new millennium (*Parent Psalm*, *Father to the Man*, *Millennium Letter* and *The England of A. R. Quinton*.) However, the mind-set within it is very much that of the mid- to late-Nineties, when I had young children, and some of the poems definitely reflect the intensity of that period of my life. Rather surprisingly, given its disparate beginnings, the material in this collection appears to have gathered around various inter-connecting themes and the title – although an obvious allusion to the context in which Edward Thomas died – extends its motif into other areas where no man's land represents the current dispensation: the joy, the pain, the uncertainty.

Fiery Hedge Publications

Fiery Hedge Information:

https://www.facebook.com/fieryhedgepoetry

www.fieryhedge.wordpress.com

Other Publications:

Nick Ware, *Perception of Light*

A second "back catalogue" volume of poetry by Nick Ware is due to be published this November.

38801017R00070

Printed in Great Britain
by Amazon

THE SUPPLANT CONSCIOUSNESS

Leslie Harrison-Fryer

First Impression, 2011

Published by LHF Books:
P.O. Box 5216,
Cardiff.
CF5 9FD

ISBN: 978-0-9571694-0-1

Printed and bound in Wales by:
Dinefwr Press Limited,
Ammanford,
Carmarthenshire.
SA18 3YD

CONTENTS

TRIBUTE

In memory of Johnny Jones who passed away before I could renew our friendship.

Very sorry and many apologies Johnny. To my endless shame I heard your call, but in the bustle of life failed to hasten to those gentle promptings of the inner voice.

Forgive me old friend, and please accept these writings as a dedication to both yourself and Howard your brother.

May you both rest in peace.

- - - the sufferings of this present time are not worthy to be compared with the glory that shall be revealed in us. For the earnest expectation of the creature waiteth for the manifestation of the sons of God.

The Apostle Paul.
Romans. 8:18-19.

FOREWORD

Interpenetrating universes and multi-conjoining dimensions may sound quite a fanciful flight of mind. That is far from the truth. Insistence that we are a single intelligent species in a single universe comprising a single three dimensional space, moving through a single plane of time is quite catatonic in its limitation and certainly a flight of fantasy.

Like helpless newborn kittens we feel our way around our basket. At the first opening of the eyes a blurred larger world seems to miraculously appear and we dream, for still we sleep. Slowly the larger world appears clearer; we mistake the table leg for a pillar to the heavens and the floor as an endless expanse. Soon we are traversing that expanse.

As many doors open, adventure beckons one or two in the litter. We visit other mansions in the house and daily we grow sturdier. Some love the basket others must move on, they can't help themselves. They eventually return with tales of wonder and of extraordinary events and happenings, but first they have to disturb and wake their sleeping brethren. The disapproving growls of dissent dismissive of such childlike enthusiasms for things afar and things anew.

THE SUPPLANT CONSCIOUSNESS

CHAPTER ONE

UPON SUCH

In the writings to follow I have sought to give witness to That which comes unto us in apparent voice. There may be no simple answer as to why some should 'hear' and others not. Often this inner Voice appears to remain silent to the robust of character and even the placid of temperament.

Its manifesting to or through the individual seems somehow linked to a certain innate confidence, a confiding trust, but in particular an unashamed, unselfconscious and willing resonance with this inner truth and reality, repeatedly revealed in some form or other to every generation. This, our concrete world of matter and phenomena suffused with another, an inner world of endlessness and mystery.

The socially saturating conventions of the Western cultures insist that this inner Voice, if heard at all, is only heard by the odd combination of the saint or the mad. Yet, it is there in each and everyone of us. None is any more privileged than another.

Even in our failings, weaknesses or attachments, it remains, forever present. For long periods this presence may appear to desert us, at other times it bubbles through into consciousness for its own noble purposes.

'Always I am with you but you see me not.'

In this statement of course no blame is levelled at mankind, for what human mind can ever come to know the vastness and entirety of the Cosmic Consciousness.

After a number of years of persistent and genuine grievance at my own lack of understanding, it was given to me that 'God is Spirit.' Not given when deep in prayer it has to be said, but when sat on a wall, shivering and awaiting transport. And upon that statement, for the succeeding fifty years or so, my mind has dwelt.

It is not so much the philosophical or theological interpretation of those particular words that is important, for the word Spirit for example, can mean so many different things to so many different people. Neither is it only about the instant luminating quality that shines in the mind's eye and ignites the receptive heart, it is also about where it takes us in thought and eventually in life.

We make the press in sincerity and questing persistence although probably in blindness, yet the Cosmic Consciousness has to answer, it cannot refuse, that is its nature, its beautiful nature.

We may rightly be suspicious of the claim that only

men and women of spotless character are given insight into the great and eternal truths and the unconveyable mysteries of the holy inner consciousness.

We may at times have been a disappointment to ourselves and to others. We may not always have been kind or patient or always had the purest of thoughts toward our fellowmen and women. Also, we may have veered from the standards advised in scripture, yet many strange and wonderful things mysteriously emanate forth into consciousness from the deep and abiding core of our inner being.

They of doctrine and creed who draw a hard line both in the heavens and in the heart, have stiff-backed straddle-legged sentinels facing the ignorant or immature proclaiming in loud voice, 'thou shalt not pass.' This anachronism we have all heard many times before and cannot simply be repeated because it has a pedigree of ecclesiastic authority.

They also, in their proclamations, have regimented sentinels facing the other way as well, demanding the same of That which is of wisdom itself. Surely this can be nought more than prided retaliation against atheists or agnostics who are hostile in their steadfast resistance mockery or even contempt. An attitude exemplified in recent history by among others, psychologist Professor R. B. Cattel who brought quote that mystical union,

'resembles the characteristics of
normal sexual consummation,'

An intellectual, taking his inspiration it seems from Bernini`s masterpiece, unashamedly assessing, through intellect alone, the reveries of the nun Teresa.

To further antagonise those of a dogmatic religious attitude Professor Cattell adds,

> 'religion has appealed especially to the inferior,
> the sick, the maladjusted, the fearful, and those
> scorned and rejected by love, power, life and society.'

These mental derivations, unworthy of comment as they may be, have been resurrected from 1938 to emphasise, even at that late date, the horrendous backlash of a boorish intellectualism released from the traps of organised suppression imposed by the Christian Church.

From within this reaction to the historically abusive church authorities sprang an overcompensating and equally denying highbrow atheism. It's this denial and atheism, among other things, that will be addressed in these writings.

We surely can't believe that millions upon millions of intelligent and sincere human beings have been, and are being fooled by a two thousand year old deluded Rabbi. Or, that all such individuals have some sort of perverse inner need or feebleness that leads them to suffer illusions of a nebulous or imagined Reality, which the hostile passionately insist isn't there.

Whatever our leanings we do have to face this fact of so many of our fellow men and women embracing wholeheartedly, not only the words of the Christ consciousness which are fresh and relevant to every generation, but also the continual existence of Being in Spirit.

The Christ consciousness lives. The Christ consciousness is alive and it is this aliveness and being (existence) that many in every culture become inwardly aware of. An active living consciousness, where there are no rituals, creeds or sects, no denominations or doctrinal attachments, be they of religion or race, country or culture. The Christ consciousness is universal and eternal.

The permeating through of this inner consciousness into the life of he who has made mistakes and probably continues to make mistakes or to he who is maybe certain of his own particular narrow reality, is always a possibility, at any time.

This appears to be the reason why, throughout history, some of the most shattering experiences have come to the most obnoxious and mercenary of men. It is not for anyone to assess who is 'good enough.' There are greater powers of Spirit than we can ever imagine.

Surprisingly this question of 'the most worthy' does seem to surface again and again even within the minds of serious forthright men of integrity. The anonymous monastic author of 'The Cloud of Unknowing' himself questions who is dearer to the Infinite, the spiritually weak or the spiritually strong. Few would seem to be of exactly the one type of character or the other. And although the story of the prodigal son may spring to mind, it must be repeated that none is more privileged than another. Love abides.

Also, the touch of the inner consciousness can embed a sense of obligation to 'That which is greater than I.' It becomes undeniable and never is that obligation questioned even within those who before, may have only followed their own will and desire.

The outer life becomes complementary to the inner. If we have no inner life or recognition of such, then the outer life has no foundation and wills as it pleases, oftimes involuntarily.

As part of his or her curriculum every schoolchild should be encouraged to read the heartrending story of a Mrs. Mary Rowlandson and her personal resolution not to attempt escape from the vengeful persecution of the North American Indians, who in frontier times, captured and imprisoned her, but to await, with patience, upon divine providence. A classic piece of writing of a childlike confidence in the Infinite, to know what it is doing, and doing in each individual life and each moment of time, be it hardship, death or rejoicing.

> 'I could not speak unto you as unto
> spiritual but as unto carnal.'
>
> The Apostle Paul

All that is written in these pages is based on the understanding that man as a species is dual in nature, he is of a sentient consciousness and he is of an inner non-sentient consciousness. He is of the material, he is of the spiritual. He is of the animal, he is of the angel. If he were not of the animal he wouldn't have access to his lineage. If he were not of the angel he wouldn't have access to his destiny.

Man has two faces, one hidden, one revealed, and as a species he primarily expresses the animal consciousness of eating, sleeping, fearing, defending and procreating. The inner consciousness is not so evident in the course of daily activity, most certainly Western social activity, where the affairs of men do seem to take too great an importance, in the affairs of men.

If there is no cognizance of anything other than the touchable, then the individual must live entirely within the confines of a mechanistic understanding and be dismissive of all else, hence the 'scientific' certainty that theirs is the only reality. That is, atomized reality 'a composition of atomic facts.' Such constriction, a living death to the mystic, and the 'corpse' of Didymus Thomas the Apostle.

If an indwelling presence is recognised as undeniable then the narrow linear world of the materialist, becomes a confining prison house. Reality invariably becomes broader, and very much of something that includes the base atomic but not solely composed of it.

Also, in our youthful everyday human life, we tend to look at the angel within, through the eyes of the flesh. Many in their later years, increasingly come to look at the flesh through the eyes of the angel, a viewpoint that appears more and more, the true heart of every man and woman, youth and child.

Even though attention will be drawn to the dangers of living circumscribed by reason, reason itself will not be abandoned in these writings, but neither will be denied or forsaken the reality of the subjective, intuitive or inspirational knowing. A knowing seeded from within the inner consciousness, a consciousness that we at present know little or nothing about, yet which can reveal or manifest at any time. Maybe for example, when a person is in deep reverence and stillness or when in sincere remorse; at the bedside of a dying friend, or undertaking a mindful daily life of non-retribution, but more surely when we witness an increasing humility within ourselves.

Unless faith is based upon an awareness of this inner consciousness or indwelling presence, then it is but belief, a belief fulfilled and realised by the first weight of insight, wonder or understanding.

The word faith, according to the dictionary, means 'belief without proof.' The word faith, for the purposes of this narrative, finds that proof within the individual human heart, alive yet without form.

Understanding, it should also be stated, has its bedrock in experience. It needs no minister, cleric or priest, no religious authority, either of creed or diktat, no culture or ceremony and no visible touchable proof or sign. And by experience, is meant, the experience as revealed unto the waking consciousness of That which never sleeps, cannot deceive or lie, is eternal, and will with great gentleness and power, touch with unbounded love, all who call either in despair, desolation or with confident yet humble longing.

Truth can never be destroyed, neither can a sincere call be refused, yet, the time of fulfilment cannot be of our own choosing, and the manner of that fulfilment cannot be of our own choosing either. It does not fail, yet has a time of its own. It has no name, and is beyond human affection or passion, which of itself may be preferential, may wane or die. There are of course many explanations why this indwelling consciousness isn't permanently channelled through us, from Lucifer influence, negative energies, pomp, pride or narcissism.

All these various explanations would probably condense down into the same thing in the end, but it does appear that the principal factor in shutting out, or overshadowing our wondrous inner consciousness, is the biologically driven, and historical unsuppressible need of primal ego to unquestioned prominence and importance.

Observe a greater reality and ego no longer contains the Universe, the Universe contains ego. Or, not only 'Thee in me' but also 'me in Thee.'

One may wonder at the power and grace of
human locomotion.
One may wonder at the dexterity of the human
hand, the imagination of the human mind.
One may wonder at the transmission of sound
to the innermost reaches of the ear, the ability
of the eye to convey beauty to the soul, or the
first faltering cry of the newborn.
One may wonder.
And praise there must be.
Sometimes for man.
But always for That
which is greater than he.

In the reading of a narrative many feel the need to know the background and even the foreground of the author. For me, the statement itself is usually enough, along with the enthusiastic dissection and digestion of any of its wisdom. However, for those who must, the manuscript 'The Plaster Room' has been written as being the early and only part of a lifetime that bears heavily on this particular commentary.

I am convinced that had not such unenviable childhood conditions existed, then these succeeding words would not have surfaced through me. That is, the conveyance that man as a species is about to be reborn. Not in any imaginary gradual evolutionary process, as is the want and so beloved of those of the status quo, but in an instant of geological time. Not of either ancient or contemporary biology but a beautiful creature of the immediate future – The Supplant.

It seems circumstances have conspired in a sort of inevitability to open up a psyche to particular, even if in certain quarters, unwelcome information. For I'm sure few can have experienced at any age, let alone so early in childhood, the long term incarceration and at times, the deep melancholy in which I unavoidably found myself for most of my early life.

This was the institutionalized background upon which I entered adult life. An early adult life of impatience, drunkenness and brawling.

Two incompatible emotions gripped me. On the one hand an ever growing, if at times painful compassion for all incarnating life, and on the other an anger that seemed to follow but one pace behind, with nearly every uttered word becoming a threat to further instil a hostile insecurity.

The attempted copying of passive behaviour proving a pretension too difficult to maintain, the anger would invariably burst through, almost blind to the consequences.

Yet always, somewhere inside, existed a certain and sure conviction that there was something more to life than the shallow spirit of grasping, ambition and possessions, something more than five sense consciousness. This ingrained conviction, a beacon I was often to ignore when inflamed and retributive. The regret at the wounding of others – crushing, the innate directness – irremissible, yet everyday demands and affairs had to be attended to.

Day by day life moved on. Slowly, ever so slowly over the years the temperamentality became less acute and the anger subsided, a more humorous view of life began to emerge. It is hard to believe that one could be born with such scarring of character.

A child who knows it has the genuine love and protection of its parents is always a joy to behold. A child torn from that early love and protection will always struggle with any reparation, for the moment of shock and loss when left with strangers at tender age, is a moment of such incurable sadness.

It is in these latter years of this incarnation that a stability, a greater equillibrium has been found. The cross, as a symbol of the all-embracing compassion of the inner consciousness has finally brought its power to bear on the stubborn storm-tossed troubled waters generated long ago in early childhood.

Generated I believe, by the ripping away and isolation from parents along with all those early years of bedridden immobility and the zealot-like enforcement of earthly regimen and authority, where even bladder and bowel were governed by the tick of the clock.

Although my own impressions have been documented, it is for the reader alone to consider how this tempestuous childhood seeded the following views, opinions and perceptions, and also the faithful acceptance of the transcendental.

It must also be stated that in the writing of this manuscript, not having to live to a professional code, does give a freedom from the inevitable strictures and impositions be they a 'singular reality' or 'accepted practices.' Whether these impositions are contractual or not, they are nevertheless always well understood within the confines of the prevailing scientific or religious culture of the time. This freedom and convenience must not be underestimated.

There are few, if any, freelance scientists for example, all are employed, and as such have to be obedient not only to the written contract of secrecy they initially have to sign wherever they work, but also to an unwritten code of convention. They are, unfortunately, as hogtied to that convention as their forefathers were hogtied to ecclesiastic conventions. Today 'heresy' in scientific circles is as dangerous to career as it was to the cleric of medieval Europe.

In any one lifetime none can expect to have in-depth knowledge of every speciality. In fact most of us, even if exceptionally curious, intelligent or innovative, only manage to study a few subjects in detail, but this should never be allowed to restrict our access to wisdom and truth from wherever it may come.

In the person of Mr. Carl Gustav Yung we have one of the most insightful psychological clinicians coming to the conclusion that the life of a Pueblo Indian, with his inner conviction, is 'infinitely more satisfactory' than the life of a man living in the Western cultures.

These are things the social constructionists would very much prefer weren`t revealed, for it does bring into question the predominant materialistic worldview of Western societies.

With all our weapons of power and the 'mass indoctrination of the all-consuming self,' we must surely ask ourselves could Mr. Yung be correct, and if so wherein lies the problem.

Is it our recent history of a seeming single minded material dynamism within our cultures, or the resignation with which many of us seem to accept without question, a life with no inner recognition and therefore no inner meaning.

Or, is it the fear, that with no inner meaning in our lives, the stripping away of our financial self-image, our things, possessions and status will not only leave us naked but also lifeless and blank. To feel so distanced and be so forgetful of our indwelling vitality that we have to weakly conclude that ultimately, we are no different to the worm, except in degree, the degree of biological complexity.

Whatever pathway in life we may be following we must always be assured that there is an inimitable and indestructible holy indwelling presence within each and every one of us, and irrevocably confirmed in every generation, in every land and every culture, past and present.

It also has to be added, that although the word holy seems to mean different things to different people, it is used here, as it is throughout these writings, to convey and emphasise the eternal and unbreachable unity of our vast inner consciousness to Deity. This inner consciousness itself, having the allegorical function of a placenta, from the greater body to the foetus, from Cosmic Consciousness to the creature.

We could also liken the inner consciousness to a web, a spider's web constructed in a meadowland, so fine and delicate that it cannot be seen in passing, except that on occasions a very brief glint or ray may catch our eye and we know it is there.

In the darkness of the night, the dew will silently settle and as the sun rises in the early morning, its radiant light, reflecting off the beaded moisture will reveal the web in all its refined wonder. Droplets of water have brought it to our knowing. Such is the revealing tear when shed in compassion.

It must also be stated that the hellfire and divine damnation so popular with those of proselytising zeal who historically dispirit more than empower, is not the future of the human race, never has been. The immediate future of the human race is a mind of impregnable integrity and a heart of undivided concern for all living creatures and all living things, and the manifesting of this vast inner consciousness, born and expressed in new flesh, in new but not dissimilar form.

Sowing and reaping is one thing but a vengeful and retributive Creative Consciousness, Universal Energy or God, flies directly in the face of my whole life experience. The panic and mortifying doubt that I may never again be worthy of the great love of the Father, of that I know. The immeasurable well of sorrow and the run from the Christ, of that I know also.

On the other hand nothing is known to me of an after death terror, torment or pain of fire and flame, oils, stones, pits or whatever. It could be such threats are but the psychological tricks of the institutional bully ensuring conformity and the accruement of worldly wealth and in turn of course, worldly power. Or, such terrors may be deliberately invoked in dream, to an errant yet receptive personality, by the inner consciousness. The intense emotion in reaction to such images, often life changing and permanent, but as dreams they are images, timely images generated by the all-knowing wisdom of the same inner consciousness.

In the Judaic Old Testament we have a fundamental retributive philosophy, 'an eye for an eye, a tooth for a tooth.' We see this urge to retribution within man, in its turn projected onto Deity. The indwelling holy presence in man contains no such retributive need, so therefore can have no need to plant retributive emotion (everlasting punishment) onto Deity. In other words, in our psychological isolation we project our earthly imperfections, limitations and character onto the Infinite.

In the New Testament of the Christ we see the eternal compassion invert this ancient instruction with a directive to non-retribution, reflecting and revealing the true spirit of the inner consciousness or indwelling presence – that first aspect of knowing. In the words of the Christ consciousness,

'All sins are forgiven unto the sons of man'

Again we witness the unbounded compassion and uncircumscribed love of the Heavenly Father, through the harmonising spirit of Jesus.

Yet, in the New Testament (a human writing of divine things) we have what is predicted by Jesus, the mixing of the old and the new. In one verse (Matt. 25:45) we have the most sublime expression of this same eternal compassion directed towards the mean of heart and mind,

> 'In as much as ye did it not to one of
> the least of these, ye did it not to me.'

Then just one verse later we have that primitive human need to retribution,

> 'And these shall go away into everlasting punishment.'

So overpowering of the human psyche is this lust to retribution that we become blind to the simple fact that hostile emotion suppressed through fear always re-remains, to at anytime explode into the outer world of men and women.

The threat and fear of punishment is all too real and forms the basis of common law. The instituting of threat and the instilling of fear will frequently result in capitulation of course, but fear itself cannot change or redeem an ugly hidden attitude – avarice, vengeance, envy, covetousness or conceit maybe. There it will remain, suppressed and festering.

Those of us who by whatever means, be it the bullet

or the book, wish to instil fear into others, retain the unkindness of lowly selfhood even if we imagine our motive to be true, in the longing for an end to war, exploitation and cruelty.

> 'He that believeth on him (The Christ) is not condemned, but he that believeth not, is condemned already.'

The word condemned and the word punishment are not interchangeable. Neither are they synonymous for they mean two different things.

If we deliberately wish to remain in blindfolds then we must surely condemn ourselves to a continuing life of ignorance. We don't in our wilfulness, indolence or even timidity instigate a merciless reaction from a Creator intent on inflicting torment, pain and distress. But never let us forget the untold numbers who have lived cowed by such unbridled and insidious inculcations.

And let us read scripture aright, namely the oft quoted words,

> 'depart from me ye cursed into everlasting fire'
>
> Matt. 25:41

These are not the words of the Christ consciousness at all, for if we begin the reading at verse 31, we see clearly, that the words are the eager imaginings of Matthew. Verses, often deliberately omitted it seems, by vengeful minds who preach their own unloving brand of scripture. And as stated, the old and the new will inevitably become mixed, and from whence all forms of hybrid or eclectic philosophies emerge.

Would the Christ consciousness ask lowly man to forgive his neighbour seventy times seven, or in other words, endlessly, if the Creative Consciousness itself was of so vengeful a nature. It doesn't make sense, even if the rational is all we have to work with. It must be remembered that biology (atrophy of the temporal lobe for example) can itself influence behaviour and limit comprehension.

To the earthbound consciousness, retribution often seems a sound ideal, and to the egocentric, a necessity. Also retribution may be seen as essential for earthly survival but is no part of the Christ spirit or consciousness, for that consciousness is not about an earthly order, it is about a heavenly order. The two are quite different. Is this the reason Paul tells us in Hebrews that Jesus despised Moses' law, or this aspect of it.

Further, in the Gospel of Matthew, 13:42 we have,

> 'And shall cast them into a furnace of fire: there shall be wailing and the gnashing of teeth.'

So overpowering becomes the passion to dictatorial finger stabbing, this verse is repeated word for word just eight verses later.

This is an obvious insertion into an original script and typifies the psychological need, and profile, of the egotistical or institutional zealot. He will take himself with him wherever he goes, be that script of a religious, political or a scientific nature.

And in Matthew 23:33 we again see a startling addition to an otherwise sober, if chastening script,

> 'Ye serpents, ye generation of vipers how
> can ye escape the damnation of hell.'

It doesn't fit in, totally out of context, and sounds very much like the fist-shaking rage of one really upset guy who has just had his washing pinched off the line. Read it without verse 33 and see what you think.

Forgiveness for those who have subjected others and possibly whole swathes of their fellowmen and women to heartless cruelty in the relentless pursuit of earthly power and dominion, is a difficult concept to accept or even understand.

The anguish and pain generated by the fulfilling of carnal ambition as it plays out in human affairs, scripture informs us, is forgiven to all, and especially to those, who in remorse, desperately yet humbly seek that love and forgiveness.

This at the heart of primary spiritual understanding and faith, and again in its revelation, part of the press that has led to the unfolding, or, the future 'issuing forth' of the Supplant on earth.

Just as the vast consciousness of the Supplant to come is incomprehensible to us, so is this essential nature, wherein such forgiveness is as lifeblood itself.

Having been at times the wildest of men, no such coming spectre of an after death vengeance has ever been revealed to me and few would request or tolerate a cuckoo land in which to live.

This mental land or maybe spiritual land of hell-fire and damnation is without reality to me, only great love and fogiveness has been my lot. I can say no other for that is how it has been.

To bring to self-reflection, to bring to remorse for the wounding of others, or regret when hard of heart, or shame at unrelenting self-will, could there be any greater power than an inescapable and saturating love.

There is much, so much we do not understand, but if this witches' brew of a hell were any part of a coming land of purgatory, then surely some aspect of it would be 'visible,' made plain and unmistakeable to the sincere or troubled heart. And anyway, even if it were true or any part of it were true, then we will suffer with fortitude the pains we may have given to others, but suffer no other to the pains that we ourselves may have had to endure.

Many who during their lifetime, have become aware of certain truths, choose to reveal them in novel form, very successful and insightful novels. Nonetheless, it is to be hoped that my untrained hand will have adequately conveyed some of the joys of the inner spirit and the ache in the human heart, without the book-seller's embellishments of romance and conflict.

With these writings it is my wish to convey personal experience, intuitive impression, deductive thought and little dogma, for others to make of what they will.

The commentary, bald of convention and uncircumvented by story and tale is as both nature and instinct have directed. Each must follow the footpath of their own calling.

CHAPTER TWO

IS ALL THIS TO BE?

'the motive power of the Universe is love, without which it would fall to pieces in a moment.'

Bhakti Yoga

With the first rays of the sun I awoke and a great love was upon me, unbounded, all-consuming. A love not of this world, not of the common passion of men and women. A love so overwhelming as to be beyond the limitations conferred by vocabulary and language.

There was no whisper of demand, no unspoken precondition and it seemed my only need was to remain wrapped and consumed in this extraordinary saturating warmth and joy.

Whatever we may think, whatever we may feel in this world of narrowness and constriction, there is an all-abiding Love in this universe.

For three days this all-pervasive love remained with me, untainted and unmixed. As my sitting body rocked to and fro in such joy and delight I became so overwhelmed by this sublime love I just could not stop the weeping. Feelings of unworthiness swept over me and the words sprang to mind,

'the heart must be washed in the blood of the soul.'

Yet the comforting presence, the enveloping love and immovable security remained with me.

I was never asked 'lovest thou me?' I felt but loved and loved greatly. A knockabout unimportant chap with lifelong infirmity, of mood and abrasion, with no discernable skill, talent or ability, shown a love that defies mortal comprehension. How could it be? It asked nothing of me, yet gave love without measure.

It was some years later, having awakened to the rural silence and early morning mists slowly meandering around house and fields, that the need to write was overpowering. Not knowing what was going to appear on the page before me, the pen was left to write as it wished.

Plough an unwavering furrow
In the ageless field of time,
To view the glorious future
Soon to enshrine mankind.

Where no mother or child sleep hungry,
Lest the whole world stand alert,
And seeds of rhythm and tranquillity
Are sown in unpoisoned earth.

Where no living thing be hunted,
No cunning, stealth or lures.
Wild birds alight on tender hand,
And protecting arm secures.

The pen continued,

Where no country need militia,
No borders to divide.
War, a distant memory.
No despots to misguide.

Where charity, love and compassion
Are link to ancestral lore.
No intent remain a secret.
Retribution is no more.

Where the Ancient of the cosmos
To each a gift will bring.
All will know their destiny.
Death will have lost its sting.

From the heavens issue forth,
Ne'er again the Father to eschew.
Man, no longer selfish renegade,
But a creature born anew.

The pen stopped and I reread the verses. From where the human race is today with its militaristic, acquisitive tribal cultures to such earthly paradise seemed an impossibility. Yet, I knew the reality of what I had experienced, such a gentle unearthly reality.

As the pen initially moved forward across the page, I read the verses as they appeared on the paper. At that first staccato reading, and at the end of the second verse the lines didn't make sense. Confused and puzzled I asked, without any feeling of abnormality or strangeness and in usual impetuous manner,

"What does that mean?"

"Write it down," came the reply.

Without further question, write it down I did.

The words just appeared on the paper before me, with hardly a thought and little correction, but where did such beautiful and moving sentiments come from. "Is all this to be?" I silently queried, hardly able to believe what had just happened, as the enormity and implication fully dawned upon me.

Such are the mysteries that surround us. Such is the wonderful breath of our inner consciousness. It comes unto us when it wishes, silently, unexpectedly and ofttimes without form. We have no power to dictate its seasons. Those who proffer delusion, understandably don't want their narrow world of tutored ignorance destabilised, such is the need to slumber at the roadside of the well trodden way.

Two episodes distanced in time, yet two profound moments in the continuity of one lifespan, which in themselves lay the foundation for the essentials of these writings.

The draw of the unknown is life itself to the visionary but poison to those of the conformist frame of mind. Yet, the sun does not refuse, in any way, to shine on either he of the vision or he of the dust.

CHAPTER THREE

THE TELLTALE ANOMALLY OF THE NEAR DEATH EXPERIENCE

What is this dieing and passing away
That haunts the tread of men.
The Lord in heaven knows the truth
But not the mind of them,
Who hurry about, rush and shout,
And are given to divers' ways.
Pause awhile, extend a hand.
Be mindful all of thy days.

As this writing is mainly featured around the contrasting aspects of consciousness within the species Homo sapiens, and to dispel certain illusions that have somehow engulfed the learned Western mind, it may be worthwhile spending a little time briefly scanning the time ordered and space oriented human consciousness, but one aspect of the duality. The known within the unknown.

The main illusion of course, being the terrible constriction that contemporary intelligentsia has placed upon the human consciousness alone. Is it any wonder, that if the lesser is denied, then how much more so, will be the greater.

'Nothing exists after death,' contends psychologist Dr. Susan Blackmore, and which could possibly read, 'of the waking consciousness nothing discernable exists after death.' For, if nothing exists after death, then to continue the logic, nothing could have existed before birth. It then follows that neither the outer nor inner conscious life of the individual, ultimately, has any inherent value, and therefore neither have ethics, compassion nor conscience. To the nihilist they become just more man-made conveniences to retain social order if not conviviality.

At some stage in each individual life the question must arise as to whether or not the ability to conscious awareness, continues after the point is reached when there is no possibility of resuscitation. Or, in esoteric terms, when the golden bowl is shattered and the silver cord is severed.

From that point on, there can only be intuitive understanding of what happens to this aspect of the individual personality, for with the irreversible stillness of the body the analytical observer has nothing to observe, and so assumes collapse or dissipation of the essential life forces and consciousness in particular.

And, while Mr. Yung instructs every practitioner within the psychological professions not to overstep scientific competence when addressing this subject, it has to be said, he comes very close indeed to disregarding his own instruction when writing of 'detached consciousness' at death, with no degree of equivocation. Mr. Yung realised that consciousness is nonmaterial and mind of independent activity.

So, psychological science (much as say geological science) plays no part in assessing what happens to the waking consciousness at transition. It is inadequate for such a task which means we must look elsewhere within ourselves, or, if the sciences are our only means of understanding, then it appears, it would have to be the highways of quantum mechanics.

It is generally accepted that the brain itself has a form of pressure valve which reacts to a sudden drop in blood pressure by releasing endorphins, morphine type substances, producing a tranquil state in what is really the beginnings of the dieing process. These endorphins (possibly linked to hypoxia) can produce the tunnel vision, bright light and feelings of well being, often experienced by those who have been in a state of clinical death, (no heartbeat, no blood pressure and no perceptible consciousness.)

It has been noticeable over the years, that those of direct experience speak the sense, while those of letter and scope seem compelled to confine that experience to their own favoured box of learning. Scientists at times, do seem to narrow down, that which they are personally unaware of, into something book-learned and earthly, whether it is the experience of the abductee, the mystic and esoteric, or the unconscious consciousness of those subjected to fevered resuscitation.

Whatever material answer the learned are inclined to pluck from their textbooks it would appear to be commonsense, that while endorphins may produce tranquillity in the dieing, they don't produce consciousness. A self-conscious 'I' hovering above the body, witness to the resuscitation, and clearly independent of the physical form and its endorphins.

It follows that this naturally induced and scientifically authenticated narcosis is biologically unnecessary, if as the materialist suggests, the process of dieing leads to total annihilation.

If there is no continuation of consciousness, it does seem foolish to produce feelings of wellbeing and calm in a creature, about to suddenly snap into nothingness.

It makes for greater intelligent appraisal and superior logic to assume that this terminal narcosis is biologically activated to ease transition in that which continues thereafter. The releasing of endorphins into an already non-functional and unresponsive brain and body only makes sense if there is something surviving, and itself capable of being selfconscious throughout the whole process we know as dieing.

If as the materialist asserts, nothing survives the dieing process then this whole business of endorphin suffusion of the brain at death is a completely valueless process, which seems very unlikely.

In the world of recuperative medicine, the use of an anaesthetic or narcotic only has value if the consciousness remains intact. It's of no use otherwise.

So, the heart has stopped, the blood pressure zero, a flat E.E.G (electroencephalograph) and possibly only a residual brain activity. The dieing process is underway with the medics working quickly to restore a heart beat. In the meantime the 'dead' patient hovers above the body and has calm and detached visual and auditory knowledge of the activity of all in the room trying to resuscitate and make the body once again fit for habitation.

The 'I' of the 'dead' patient is present and fully aware. The 'I' consciousness can peer into the world of the atom and witness **EVENTS,** not the chemical, magnetic or electrically induced images of the neuro-scientist, but events. Many in the professions of theory and experiment, feel compelled to insist that these out-of-body experiences are biologically based, in attempt to swing everything back to a materialistic format.

These intelligent folk must know that biology itself cannot be responsible for this out-of-body conscious reality, regardless of any tunnels, light or euphoria, yet like automatons, keep repeating the same old stuff year in and year out.

Knowledge of the material world cannot be gleaned by those who are unconscious or clinically dead, unless of course there is another non-physical dimension to human consciousness. An alternative way of knowing, independent of the five physical senses and under certain circumstances (or maybe any circumstance) able to 'see' into the physical world.

These patients reveal, upon reawakening, details the medics know could not have been obtained through the everyday conscious means of perception. Nursing staff are aware that something out of the ordinary is taking place which they are unable to explain, and for professional reasons choose to remain silent. The jumpy traditionalist awaiting surgery, wouldn't want a perceived scatter-brained nurse about the place, with questionable ideas, and her head in the clouds.

The stilled heart and the dieing brain, with its closed extremities, cannot see and be witness to the urgent activity of medical or surgical resuscitation, no more than can the earlobe or kneecap.

Conversely, there are those who have 'died' and have had no conscious knowledge of resuscitation or anything else. Mr. Kerry Packer, reputed to be Australia's richest man at the time, 'died' for some eight minutes. After resuscitation he commented,

"I've been there and there is nothing."

What, we may ask, is the determining factor in this awareness that some have, when obviously unconscious in the conventional sense, while others remain in blackout. A difficult one to answer. We often have a result before we have a reason.

If we can still think and observe when clinically deceased, then it obviously means consciousness is independent of a brain, dead to the physical world. To avoid accession to such truth and the inevitable implosion of materialism, we have this continuous adolescent refrain, of the dogmatic belief in a single world of matter and a single conscious understanding of that, and nothing else.

Similarly, for telepathy to take place, the linear thinker will argue that the brain would have to produce a far greater energy output on transmission, to enable a faraway brain to receive. The same or similar bi-polar processes, at a non or subatomic level that produce the connectedness of one mind to another, are also active when the consciousness, stationed above the inert body, is witness to resuscitation.

Consciousness is of the whole brain we are told, yet when that brain is completely split into two, physically, surgically split (which on occasions is a medical necessity) having no contact one side with the other, the conscious 'I' remains in no way diminished.

The brain is a material object, a body part (60% fat) and remains of the same matter, whether its 'owner' is at one second alive or the next second dead. Except, that blood no longer flows and begins to congeal. Nobody would suggest that our awake consciousness is generated by lung, spleen or pancreas, then why cling to something equally as daft, that human consciousness is generated by the brain, by fat.

Neither can thought be generated by the brain, maybe through the brain, but not by the brain, for intelligence cannot be created by matter. The cellular imprint of intense emotion or instinct is of course something quite different. A passive recording rather than an active generation.

Many of qualification, in their rigidity of self, do insist most passionately that all consciousness is generated by matter, the brain. In their certainty they very much parallel those of yesteryear, when in their restricted mindset, insisted and tutored that matter only existed in two states, solid and liquid, and this even after witnessing vessels blown to bits by air pressure alone. The invisible, similarly escapes today's learned, yet like their ancestors they seem to leave themselves in no doubt that they are correct in their false assertions.

Also, the identical twin who actually witnesses the demise or accident of its troubled birthpal, even though he or she may be many miles or thousands of miles away, cannot see such happenings with the physical eyes or any other organ of the body. The same can very much apply to mother and child.

An unbiased appraisal of the near death experience tells us that human consciousness and thought are inextricably linked. Although the power of thought has its roots in consciousness, consciousness does not have its roots in the brain. Without matter, consciousness remains in potential; without consciousness, matter remains without form.

As human consciousness, has at minimum, a bi-polar component, not obvious to our five sense cognition, so it would appear that thought is also subject to this same bi-polar component. On the surface of things we would expect thought to be non-existent without the time to have thought, as we psychologically expect consciousness to be nonexistent when the body is clinically dead.

The near death experience and its out-of-body awareness convince us that things are not as we conclude from deduction alone, and, that the power to thought is also continuous.

The body and brain, inert and unresponsive to external stimuli and the time-based activities around the body itself. Yet, thought and consciousness continue in detached form, detached that is from all normal means of physical and psychological sensibility, cognition and comprehension.

Psychologists who seek to compress the near death experience into the cocked-hat of rationality, fail to address the main issue of how, for example, the lifelong blind when totally unconscious and clinically dead, looking from above, are able to see their own body for the first time, and even able to see details of the outside world which they have never seen before, as well as the complex surgical instruments used in theatre.

Mainly because of the present excellent and speedy resuscitation techniques, there are now so many individual cases of these so-called near death experiences, few would doubt their authenticity, but with no reasoned answers to the phenomena, inadequate explanations are bound to pop up.

Even if the mechanics of a bi-polar shift in consciousness can be explained by quantum physics or quantum theory, consciousness itself still remains illusive to explanation. The complexities of consciousness are sufficient to keep the most probing and inquisitive temperaments, occupied indefinitely.

And until those of science have grasp of the fundamental interaction between nonmaterial consciousness and material perception, then it is only sensible to admit that science itself, cannot tell us anything of the life that follows death.

Who can doubt for one moment that the near death experience and its conscious knowledge are anything but factual. That an awareness of the world of the atomic can be real without the body being in an awake state.

And whatever the detail or capacity of the individuality which 'sees' into our world, it has a knowing of time and space, even though itself not of it.

One specialist who has revealed some of the many inexplicable happenings around the time of transition, is coroner Dr. Janis Amatuzio M.D. In a sensitive writing 'Forever Ours' Dr. Amatuzio conveys the evident continuation of consciousness beyond the immediate dying hours. Not a writing to be missed by anyone interested in the subject of consciousness and its various manifestations.

During a lifetime career in neurology and neurosurgery, a Dr. Wilder Penfield operated on hundreds of individuals suffering epileptic seizure, having to probe, with electrodes, deep into the convolutions of the brain while ensuring patients remained conscious. The brain itself, as explained by Dr. Penfield, does not give rise to pain, which makes such conscious invasive surgery possible.

From his unique surgical experience it appears that Dr. Penfield is convinced that mind activity is independent of the neuronal impulses within the brain. The present scientific belief, is as already stated, that mind and therefore consciousness, is but a function of the brain, a product of matter.

Dr. Penfield throughout his commentary 'The Mystery of The Mind' retains a careful hesitancy, yet makes significant contribution to mind being of 'different essence' to the brain, by telling us that it is 'absurd' to believe that the brain, on its own, can carry out the functions of mind.

Is the conscious human mind, in its complexity, not only a directing force influencing and utilising the automatic human responses or reflexes, but also a photographic type receptor, taking impression and also instructing recall through the channel of a two-way fleshly mechanism within the brain.

To block that two-way fleshly channel, by epileptlc seizure or external electrical impulse, disallows the mind to manifest itself or to function through the brain. But significantly, mind remains intact and unaltered, for when the blockage (the electrical impulse for instance) is removed and the fleshly channel restored, mind once again is realised, and can once again manifest in the world of the atom, with memory in no way impaired, diminished or lost.

The photographic type impression on mind, derived from the neuronal impulses of open-eyed consciousness, does not in general, seem able to manifest through the brain mechanism into the external world, if the neuronal imprint within the brain itself, has been damaged or destroyed. Yet the mind memory remains, unerasable, both in life and beyond it seems, as does its vital energy and independent activity.

As the mind is a directing force, it is sensible to ask, from where does it receive its energy to generate that motivation. The rationalist will tell us from the brain itself, yet others will say from some source other than the dense matter of cell, blood and nerve-bundle.

One doesn't have to be a religionist to be of this latter persuasion, for the separate essence of mind, actively independent of the brain, is now a valid hypothesis in the science of neurophysiology. The energy source of the mind, whether presumed to be independent of the brain or not, is presently unknown to science.

As the brain is but an instrument in the scheme of things, so is the mind. Then who, we may ask, is using these instruments. The neuroscientist can only take individuality as far as mind, a valuable step indeed, but then incorrectly assumes that mind and 'I' are one and the same.

The esoteric has always informed us that mind has a causal capacity of its own, the brain being but a neural base, a neural functionary through which mind can manifest that causal capacity. An observation that is presently being given greater attention in scientific circles. Here, we are referring to the mind itself, and not its possible gravitation or attraction to purity or otherwise.

The mind as a single finger of causal and conscious expression, extending into the realm of matter from an inner consciousness. This personal observation but a continuation of the observations relayed by Dr. Penfield. Further, it is suggested that these incarnating fingers of conscious fragments do not perish with the death of the body but live eternally and all at once, within the vastness of the inner consciousness, incomprehensible to our daily linear successive rational thought processes. Is the birth of the sparrow a perpetual existence?

Let us also, briefly compare our cognitive conscious life for a moment with the dream state and begin with an interesting if unusual question, 'Is it possible to opt out of the dream while still dreaming?'

That is, to stand aside and as a witness from outside the dream, as it were, to observe the dream for what it is. In the dream state we are aware and thinking, yet unaware of our normal everyday world.

The 'I' lives the dream intensely which we know is unreal, just as the 'I' lives intensely when in the awake state. If, when in the dream, we don't know it is unreal, then could we be equally misjudging about the 'solid' world in which we live, when awake.

If we were but a witness when dreaming, then the dream of course could not hold us with the tenacious and sometimes terrifying grasp it does, and neither, it is suggested, could the awake state similarly hold us slavishly in its enthrall.

Is a dream of any concrete importance in itself? It may be the product of avoided or suppressed emotion and entirely subjective, but in itself we know it is not solid, it is as insubstantial as the projected flat screen picture in the cinema. Could we ask the same question of the reality of the everyday.

There may be many differences between the 'real' world and the dream world, but could the fundamental difference be one of language, with the dream speaking to us in symbol and metaphor and only in honesty.

We could also ponder the question, who or what designs our dreams, for they appear to be of intelligent creation, even if at times a little confusing. We are duped into believing the pictures created are real, believing as real that which has no substance.

We may, with determination, seek to be consciously aware of the dream while dreaming. If we are unready for such, then the dream first of all convinces us that we are awake, although we are not. Side-stepping our efforts, it retains its vigour and dynamic. We seem powerless in the face of such overwhelming intelligence and its apparent unremitting grasp. On waking we realise we have been fooled once again and in probable frustration snap a pencil. Only later, with increasing humility, do we realise what a wonderful and benevolent guide it is, that influences our maturing.

And even though psychology, as a science, will acknowledge that dreams are from another dimension, short sighted and earthbound psychologists still look to biology, to flesh, to fat, as the basis for the conception, generation and manifestation of the dream.

For many years, just before sleeping, we may make

the nightly statement 'I will remain conscious when dreaming.' The moment will eventually arrive when we are fully asleep, yet fully conscious that we are dreaming. We are consciously aware that we have a sleeping body and also consciously aware that we are 'in' a dream. The flat two-dimensional, apparently colourless pictures become vivid, the detail of full colour and three-dimensional.

We are not looking in from outside (as we do with a picture book,) we are fully within the dream, moving from scene to scene, yet completely aware that this 'reality' is dream reality, and so, no longer threatening or stressful. We look intensely at those who speak to us, aware that they are dream people, the clothes they wear are dream clothes, the garden dream garden. We consciously survey the now unimpingeing dream not as distressing but to some degree, entrancing.

Instead of the dream events, appearing as actually happening to us, we now walk through them with dispassion and no rush to return to the sleeping body. Fascinated instead of assaulted.

Astounding as it is initially, this conscious awareness when in dream, doesn't appear to be the natural state of the Homo sapiens, as it is not easily repeated.

If, to the indwelling presence, our carnal world and mortal circumstance have a dream-like appearance or nature, then maybe the spotlight importance we attach to the earthly reality when embedded in it, is equally misplaced. As could be the fear we attach to the passing out of the material dream, or dieing,

If, when we awake, we remember a dream and wish to return into it, to maybe square up to the bully in our newfound confidence, are we able? It doesn't seem so.

Sir Oliver Lodge and a few others of the Spiritualist Movement did say that after they died they would make every effort to contact those left behind, to prove the existence of life after death. It appears no satisfactory contact was made by Sir Oliver or his companions after passing away. This does not negate the Spiritualist Movement, for many genuine and inexplicable things do happen in séance rooms.

As it is very difficult, if not impossible, to return into the dream once we are out of it, is it equally as difficult to return into the 'dream' of earthly life. And as the eternal life of the inner consciousness is our true abode and vitality are we asking the wrong or not so important question anyway. Shouldn't we be more absorbed with 'that which lies within' in all its eternal vastness, and not so much the conscious fragment of creaturely living. In other words, are we but looking at a facet of the diamond and mistaking that breathtaking facet for the diamond itself.

We are informed that matter is not solid, yet there is no doubt that to our human cognition, the world of matter does appear to have a sure and solid reality, as does the dream at the time it is happening. Of the spiritual and unbounded, it is apparent that our narrow and circumscribed five sense perception is not revealing things as our spiritual self sees them.

If we could in our awake state, through meditation, contemplation, reflection, stillness, prayer or anything else, view things in the same way as this indwelling presence views things, then our whole centre of awareness would shift, dramatically. We would then be viewing the dreamlike nature of the awake state as we view the phantasmal like nature of the dream state, when 'out of it.'

This gravitation would be an enormous and profound leap in perspective and comprehension. A single step that in itself would traverse untold boundaries and unshackle man from his courageous if troubled existence in the temporal world of the limpet like attachments into which he is born.

Raising our eyes to a bright blue sky, a beautiful white swan enters our vision. It forms itself into a circle with its head at the centre. Looking through a glass panelled door from inside a room, and through a large shrub on its outside, a white, now vertical form is glimpsed through the bush which contains its offspring.

The white figure silently glides away and the longing to follow is intense. The door is barred with laths of timber nailed in place. As the timber strips are removed from the door with some ease, the thought may cross our mind that a more impenetrable job could have been done with screws.

Even so, anxiety grips us, as any delay in removing

the timber laths could mean the direction in which to follow will be lost. The metaphor and symbol of dream in the form of pictures, intelligently expressing something extremely profound and urgent.

To follow after the Christ, we are being informed, is not difficult, for the barriers across the door are easily removed, but they have to be removed, that is the implication. Within the secular life we lead, how do we identify those barriers. The barriers (plural – laths) that remain, are simply and solely, attachments to the worldly and temporal, and servility to the demands of body and ego.

As we unerringly grow from childhood into greater physical maturity, so it would seem, we grow into a greater maturity of spiritual understanding, including the knowledge that we have existence beyond the confines and vicissitudes of human form. Yet, the forcing of non-attachment, through will alone, doesn't seem sound, for when the time is right, non-attachment seems the most natural of processes, a delight in itself and not a hardship of grit and determination. The scales of dead skin falling from the body, while renewal takes place naturally. Our heart will always follow the love that lies within it.

CHAPTER FOUR

FURTHER TO THE DUALITY

'the physical make up of the brain
programmes us to believe in God.'
Author unknown

Another speculative statement designed to negation, to convince that spirituality is fabrication, self-delusion or matter generated. The atheistic assumption pre-exists before the statement is made and can readily be viewed as emanating from the parietal lobe – the rational and analytical. For if the temporal lobe is the seat of inner expression, then the parietal lobe is the seat of the analytical, and that has to be balanced to some degree otherwise we are no more than an upright animal, even though of vocabulary, erudite and adorned with silk finery.

It does seem that with little or no temporal lobe activity the brain is only half alive and the individual spiritually senseless. We then have the situation where those qualified in the material sciences feel it necessary to comment upon things they know nothing about or have never experienced.

It appears that the esoteric or indwelling is not experienced by those with no ear to hear, or in other words, limited temporal lobe activity or function, although ego, certain that its rationality is able to be all-knowing, will inform us of something quite different.

The physical make up of a healthy brain cannot programme belief in anything. The brain is but a conduit through which flow the waters of life.

Yet, could it be that shortcomings in the physical brain are responsible for an unbalanced materialistic outlook. Initial experimentation and brain scans do strongly suggest this to be so. From these results, materialism as a philosophy appears to be the consequence of physiological malfunction, or atrophy of the temporal lobe. The lesser the activity of the temporal lobe the greater, it seems, the obsession with materialism where the physical world and its functioning completely preoccupies the individual.

Casting more smoke screens, we have mystical experience classified in similar circles as temporal lobe epilepsy. During such transcendental moments of illumination, the individual is in a state of heightened consciousness and is not unconscious as is the epileptic.

Again we have to be suspicious of 'scientific' phraseology or misnomer, for it does appear that the word epilepsy has been carefully and deliberately chosen and adopted by corporeal temperaments in order to deny that which cannot be understood by the earthbound. The transcendental – a hateful intrusion into an otherwise ordered if narrow existence and less distressing if understood as sickness or hallucination.

Those who insist that there is another element or

dimension running through all earthly life, willingly admit of mysteries to which they have no reasoned answers. But one thing they do seem certain about is that reason and logic have limitation to understanding.

That awareness of such things, as the transcendental, the mystical and esoteric understanding, can only be arrived at through a combination of both temporal lobe and 'heart,' metaphysical centres of non-rational awareness, agreeing with Dr. Albert Einstein, who readily informs us, that it is the mystical from which springs all true science. The mystical, that is, not the rational.

And yet science would have us believe that its various interpretations are but one piece of seamless cloth. This isn't so, for while we are passionately assured by Professor Richard Dawkins, 'the paranormal is bunk,' Mr. Gustav Yung informs us that it is only through the religious experience that we are made whole, with the science of psychology being but a guiding hand pointing the way. Not so much a rend in the cloth it seems, but a different cloth altogether.

Further, is it sensible for any, learned in the sciences, to legitimately claim that all transcendental or mystical experience is organically generated by the brain, in attempt to localise or even denigrate and devalue that experience. The wider existence of an ungraspable inner consciousness is anathema and an abhorrence to he of nought but the rational as guide.

To avoid pandemonium in ego, the obvious has to be denied, continuously denied, again of course with smile and good manner as if these endearments were themselves convincing arbiters of truth.

When we address the spiritual, we address a different order of things and that order cannot be understood by the deductive analytical processes alone. If we try to assess the spiritual with just the intellect then the results are rarely anything but erroneous.

It's saddening indeed, to witness the ignorance of our own inner finings and the rampant need to think answers, to solid answers, to science answers.

It does appear that our inner consciousness needs an active centre in the brain to be able to reveal, to manifest, and our highly intelligent chums just happen to have a languid receptive centre or inactive temporal lobe(s). Therefore this primary consciousness is never experienced, never witnessed, and as such can have no personal reality, which of course leads to the self-certainty of its non-existence.

The timeless inner consciousness, a reality beyond our own with the potential to infiltrate our everyday awake state. Very much the antithesis of the narrow minded and incorrect view that all consciousness and thought is made or manufactured by flesh, that intelligence is borne of matter.

Because this inner reality cannot be conjured by reason, is unresponsive to demand, not quantifiable and its manifestations not repeatable to order, it remains anathema to the materialist of no intuitive input, however well educated in the sciences.

Also, it could sensibly be asked, if this primary consciousness is so unimaginably vast, then even in this new species, all the darker forces must still be there to live and manifest in the physical world.

From a purely logical point of view, the question seems impregnable in its suggestion that any such coming Supplant will also be subject to the same 'selfish stain' as man. Undoubtedly, every aspect of the unbounded inner consciousness will remain, but without egocentricity, these so called 'powers of darkness' will have no means or vessel through which to express and so remain only as a universal potential, in as much as 'the Devil be bound.'

Ultimately, all consciousness is one. Yet in human form, that of section and sequence, time and moment, do appear independently real, and it is from that standpoint or conditioning that the duality, expressed in these writings, is observed. Although no aspect of consciousness can ever be separate or isolate, its manifestation has multifarious form.

If we could suspend the faculty of perception for a moment, would the sense of separateness leave us and a greater sense of unity prevail. Is perception by its very nature but a metaphorical prism. If so, then the mystic of each and every age must be correct, when telling of the indivisible unity of all life and all things.

The disclosed remote viewing undertaken by Intelligence Services worldwide also shows if nothing else, a psychic ability not yet understood. That is, beyond the ordinary, or in other words, paranormal. We shouldn't feel uncomfortable with the unknown and fearfully withdraw into our own familiar territory, because after all, that is what non-selfconscious birds, animals and insects do instinctively.

It is true that more than half the population of the Western world have personal experience of what they would describe as the paranormal, at some stage in their lives. Something private, something intense, something eternal, outside five sense experience, non-mortal, non-scientific, irrefutable. A harder nut to crack than many in their materialistic convictions would ever suppose, and anyway, has been tried by all manner of men throughout the ages with no lasting success.

The obsession with denial and ludicrous speculation as to how everything scriptural or transcendental can be explained away by professors in laboratories with their farcical theories and limiting gadgetry.

And again among the intelligentsia there will always be those who with inexhaustible persistence, deprecate all things paranormal, because they themselves it appears, have no comprehension of such, feel no wonder at such and see no beauty in such. A one-eyed man can never be master in a land of bilateral vision.

When Mr. Dean Radin, parapsychologist at the University of Nevada, produces the profound work that he has and titled that work, 'The Conscious Universe' we know the rigid physical basis upon which science has been founded, is just too restrictive. It should obviously be based on a much broader foundation.

Through instrumental, verifiable and repeatable experimentation, Mr. Radin has proved the existence of precognition. In other words the existence of the paranormal. But more important than this, is the obvious fact that matter itself, the brain mass in particular, cannot of itself anticipate or predict the future. That can only come from a consciousness independent of matter. And from these persuasive results science has potential for immediate expansion, if the strangulating grasp of close-minded materialism within the professions can be released a moment, by embracing the reality; that although entwined, there is a separateness of consciousness and body matter.

It could be suggested that the unremitting need to denial of all but the earthy, can readily be compared to the self-centred certainty of Spinoza,

> 'In these propositions I have explained
> the nature and properties of God.'

Was it something other than the observation of the apparent transitory movement of the sun across the sky that would make the thinking man of antiquity, assume that the earth was the centre of the Universe, the centre of creation, and that every planet and sun in existence moved about him. Could it be exactly the same egotism that assumes but a finite singularity of consciousness. Both assessments are of course primitive, the one exposed, the other still culturally entrenched.

We are also informed that science,

> 'reverses the old ontological argument
> for the existence of God.'
>
> Professor R. B. Cattell

The systemic complexity of the atomic world, of both the microscopic and the cosmological, far from reversing the argument for the existence of a higher power, is more and more reinforcing that position, even if not witnessed transcendentally. And, not as in the past through any primitivism or communal fear of the elements or spirits, but by the combination of an inner awakening linked to the considered conclusions obtained through reason and deduction.

The sciences themselves, when free of politics, the stain of arrogant personality and external fund control, become drivers to a greater and greater certainty of some sort of inscrutable creative power of incalculable and inconceivable depth and breadth.

That it be inscrutable to the intellect, but visioned by the childlike is more than an irritant to many a cultural sophist. Even the present pain of loss, we somehow think is our own, yet was evident many hundreds of thousands of years ago, for we are told the Neanderthal laid their dead on a bed of petals before covering with more petals.

We have to put our prided social complexity into more humble perspective, for the need and utilization of, say, the most advanced fighter bomber, is exactly the same need and utilization, by elementary peoples, of the bow and arrow.

To consider such improvement of implement, tool or weapon as evolution is misguided, in that the reasoning or analytical potential or capacity of the Homo sapiens hasn't changed since inception. It's understandable we wish to think of ourselves as superior to our ancestors even if it isn't the case. Had the Homo sapiens no combative capability to wound or to kill and no desire for dominion, then neither the bow and arrow nor the multi-purpose military jet aircraft would have ever existed.

Over the years and throughout history there has been a visible inability of the spiritually blind, to crush and sweep clean from the culture, the spiritual impulse of the inner reality or even the inner reality itself.

From the first days of the industrial revolution and even earlier, the air of desire and expectation through the new found sciences never did find its total fulfilment, nor could it.

Even the irreligious idealism, in the early years, within the science of psychology has undertaken a certain mellowing or reversal with time. For to some who entered this study, their first unabashed aim it appears, was to seek a diagnosis that spiritual worship was the result of illusory imagination and invention. Governed by a damning need, they failed to see in themselves the delusions they sought in others.

Mr. Carl Gustav Yung has himself expressed certain reservations about the non-scientific or non-reasoned field of the metaphysical. In line with his personal metabolism Mr. Yung explains that the symbolism of the metaphysic conveys no understanding to him, so by pursuing the processes of psychology he follows a similar path and has similar experiences.

Mr. Yung can only 'push aside' the metaphysical and its esoteric revelations. Although a master of the symbol Mr. Yung states the symbols of the metaphysic leave him without understanding. (The Secret of the Golden Flower) To search for an alternative way through psychology, encompasses a greater degree of insight and interest, unlike the impatient dismissal when left cold by what appears to be mumbo-jumbo, much as others are left cold, by lack of understanding of ritual and ceremony, its attire, regalia and procession, whether it be Black Rod or the gilded carriage.

While some may only see the esoteric as the fertile field of the charlatan, Mr.Yung in his greater breadth of understanding knew many he had met, were truthful in what they were telling him, but he needed the experience within his own honest frame of reference and reality. The mainly Eastern practitioners of this metaphysic, an esoteric reality rather than the 'theory' of dictionary, he concludes, are really 'symbolic psychologists' and of course, not to be taken literally.

Those of symbolism invariably find the world of mental quiet, stilled reflection and silence more exalting than logic and continuous and unending activity.

Give me a moment of silence
Where others may ask for fame.
Just the tell of the silence
To ease my heart once again.
The balm to carry us onward
Through the rip of the storm.
Enter my soul ephemeral friend
Boundless, still, without form.

To the literal mind ('why don't you just say what you mean') the hurdles to understanding the metaphysic and symbol are not hurdles at all but a foreign language. The 'symbolism metaphysic' often has similar terminology to the poetic, it is of that particular comprehension and uplifting expression, which is why the great physician has to record that his repudiation is not agnosticism or against a trust in a higher power. To he who has no heart for the metaphysic he can have no head for it either. There are many routes across an ocean, or the 'trackless way' as Byron puts it.

In the training rooms of contemporary social counsellors, it seems the writings of Mr. Yung are given short shrift, possibly because he deliberately draws attention to the predominant materialistic mindset of Western cultures, aware as he was of the inevitable mental, emotional and even physical ill-health that often follows such one-sidedness. A one-sidedness Mr. Yung denounces as barbarous.

However sharp the spear; it can never penetrate the blind mat of illusion. Illusion, fostered by the narrow ego-view, and fortified by a carnal need that seeks surety within the confining boundaries of its own perceptions.

Obviously one cannot deny the ego-view in its entirety, but what is expressly denied in these writings, is the exclusivity of an external world of matter and a single conscious understanding of that.

Our everyday outer consciousness can seem like a well tended garden, it's familiar and we use it continuously without question, whereas the inner consciousness we consider as some far off distant land we have been told about in one fairy tale or another.

"Man is lived by the It" exclaims rebel physician Mr. Georg W. Groddeck. Again we see the conscious awareness of the duality. Even if we don't segment the statement into its component parts, the essentials of the duality are vividly highlighted in so penetrating and brief a statement.

Mr. Groddeck is referring to the vast indwelling presence ('a wondrous force') and he has expressed things as well as can be expressed with words. And yet it is an impossible concept to be understood by the intellect. It can only be known of the heart.

There is nothing wrong of course with the development of the intellect, providing we have a balancing spiritual insight. Psychology informs us that the Western world has an unbalanced development, as have parts of the world with the obverse – an immature intellect.

Yet, when intellect stands alone, aloof, defiant, haughty and superior, poetry for example becomes 'permitted' by that intellect, while rhyme is deemed to be nought more than 'primitive animism.'

In contradiction, it has to be stated that there is value in animism to the essential stability and wholeness of the human mind. The child who secretly pilfers a chocolate biscuit in full view of her teddy bear and with finger to pursed lips, entreats the bear to remain silent, may once again be bringing attention to our own lost joy of the 'vision splendid.'

While animism may be unappealing to the adult Western mind, we should not be dismissive of such, for there are, as already stated, deep pitfalls and potential sickness in both mind and body, of living entirely worshipful to the princes – logic and reason. An unspoken and even unrecognised apotheosis.

The rationalist, who cannot 'see' that the flower opens to the sun to feel the warmth upon its face, presents a difficult problem indeed to those who have an unending need to colour in the pictures.

The esoteric or mystic will state,

'Be still and know that I Am'

We are tenderly drawn into the impersonal world of the Eternal. But no, the rationalist reads the statement and is compelled to conclude that it is incomplete, so sets to work.

In his frustration with a perceived incoherence, he reasons that the 'I' must refer to the Infinite so the statement is 'completed' with the additional words 'thy God.' The statement now has all the hallmarks of the finger wagging autocrat and in the process loses its timelessness and endless mystery. The 'God' of the rational once again prevailing in its distortion.

In this one instance alone we can readily contrast the gentle promptings of the mystic with the assertive and destructive addition of the authoritarian.

The natural contemplative receives great joy from the fathomless mystery of the inner life. The fundamentalist, whether autocratic or not, obtains fulfilment in recruitment, the pyramid of organising power and attachment to the minutiae of the written word.

If there were no personal or militaristic gain in the use of both reason and logic, one does wonder if they would be so revered, capitalised and culturally embedded, even to the extreme extent where one contemporary professor sees the 'ultimate triumph of reason' as 'knowing the mind of God.' Such statement reinforces the observation that a professorship doesn't necessarily give us grasp or insight into the transcendental – that which transcends reason.

And, it is not the suppression of reason that is called for, but its extension, to include the reality, that the spiritual is the foundation and core of our being, while the physical, the material, is but appendage.

The inner consciousness is largely unfathomable to the cognitive. And, as the cognitive has an innate limitation of comprehension, it is inevitable that the rational will seek to make substance of the Spirit. A tendency to freeze in form the formless.

The traditional seminary existed long before the advent of the New Testament, emphasising this age-old and continuous need to attempt the capture of Spirit in vessels of creed and ritual, as it silently moves through the very gene of life, and through the whole body of the seen and unseen cosmos.

As a pail of seawater can tell us little or nothing of the heave and swell, the still and thunder of the open ocean, so neither can alabaster, monument, ritual or icon tell us but little or nothing of the agelessness and endlessness of the Infinite. Have faith, pleads the Christ, yes truly, have faith.

To conclude this chapter, we can readily observe that the assimilation of the new or unfamiliar, inevitably leads to denial of the outworn or outgrown, however culturally saturating or socially iconic those practices may be. For example, the obsession with success and its veneration, the affliction of ambition and the nurturing of competitive instinct, the possessive protection of good reputation and its value to career, the will to affluence and its profane show, along with the passion to acquisition And then there is the hunt for privilege and closely guarded elitism.

In their gaining or retention by will alone, a train of opposing forces are unavoidably set in motion. Man cannot live solely by the fulfilment of mortal ambition and the steeping of his life in just reason and logic, it will invariably drive him mad.

The questioning and uncertainty welling up in those who have previously accepted the culturally indoctrinated norms – the conventional wisdom of the day, is probably the very beginning of this process of increasing awareness of a self-conscious duality.

Oh conscious life,
are you real
or are you dream.
You become, only
to pass into memory.
Timeless memory
that can fade in flesh,
or wither in disease.
Oh conscious life,
in thine own
unbecoming,
thou doest breed
the discontent
of which man in his appetite
is so filled.
The grand passing
of your every moment
an obituary,
your every moment to come
a promise.
Oh conscious life
make me but one promise,
that thou wilt show forth
the Permanence
of ancient lore.
If this one request
is not thine to grant,
then begone,
I will seek elsewhere.

CHAPTER FIVE

THE RABBI JESUS

`Tis true my form is somewhat odd
Blaming me is blaming God.
Could I create myself anew
I would not fail in pleasing you.
If I could reach from pole to pole
Or grasp the ocean with a span
I would be measured by the soul.
The mind's the standard of the man.
Joseph Merrick (the elephant man)

From imported misconception we are informed that he, who has lifelong infirmity, has such affliction because of transgression in a previous incarnation. A viewpoint echoed in a question by the disciples,

'Master, who did sin, this man or his
parents, that he was born blind.'
(John 9:2)

to which Jesus replied,

'Neither has this man sinned nor his parents.'

We must remember, the man was born blind so the

question must relate to pre-existence.

Joseph Merrick, although physically disfigured has captured so beautifully in verse the blessed expression of the vital indwelling presence which has come to us Westerners most vividly through the words of Jesus Christ.

Scriptural writings contain testament to the inner consciousness in contrast to that of the everyday cognitive intelligence. It is this scriptural confirmation of the duality that we now need to consider.

Even in everyday conversation or debate of the scriptural, we see this duality surfacing. On the one hand we have an ever increasing impersonal and transcendental Christ, while on the other, Jesus has become just another ordinary sort of guy who 'ascended the Mount of Temptation and for forty days and nights did sit and think about the wrongs he saw in his society.' An excruciating statement from within the commentary of a television documentary.

Or, Jesus is seen as a family man with numerous offspring, or even as a politically leaning rabble-rousing socialist initially ducking condemnation by the Roman occupiers, with the words 'render unto Caesar.'

To the conservative of British politics he becomes a capitalist, for the Good Samaritan we are told, had wealth and without wealth we can't have social services. How scripture becomes contorted into whatever our opinions demand. To others he was a fanatical or psychopathic altruist, a wayward illegitimate or an epileptic. To psychologist Mr. Binet Sangle, Jesus was,

> 'a religious maniac with visual, auditive,
> verbal kinaesthetic, verbalautomic and
> aeroplanic hallucinations.'

Whatever that lot may mean, we must agree, it doesn't sound very encouraging.

It has also been stated that the Jesus of scripture was a Gentile although of Jewish tradition and that he lacked humour. Surely in his greeting to Nathanael we can see him wryly smile as he comments,

> 'Ah, an Israelite without guile.'

Yet to others, the whole of scripture becomes some sort of antediluvian stage play and the Gospels themselves 'mythological narratives.'

Because this holy man Jesus, healed on the Sabbath and questioned the will to vengeance, it may make him, in a superficial way a religious rebel, as stated by Mr. Yung. It does however indicate that not even Mr. Yung had grasped the full enormity of the inner consciousness and its blinding expression in Jesus Christ. It was overwhelming to the laity about him and inherently threatening to those of episcopal power, with little but formality and ritual to support themselves.

Worming our way into the mind of the Jewish priesthood of two thousand years ago, we witness a repugnance for this wandering Rabbi. The well-heeled hierarchy with Ciaphus and Annus at its head, bitterly resented this outsider, not only questioning traditional temple practices, but incredulously inverting the basic Mosaic tenet to retribution.

The fulfilment of Jewish scripture in the personage Jesus Christ, the Jewish people have never accepted. It is quite understandable when the foundation of that scripture – 'an eye for an eye' is not only cast aside but a diametrically opposed, and infinitely more difficult instruction advocated.

Reacting predictably to the provocation of the Christ and his table-turning, a seething Jewish priesthood unaware of how they were being drawn into the unfolding events of an historical drama of unparalleled proportions.

It does seem trite to make statement that the Rabbi Jesus was no ordinary man. With little or no self concern, he sought to deflect attention from himself onto the Infinite. He was especially born, with an express purpose to his life, that purpose emanating from Divine Mind.

The prevailing opinion that Jesus was a young man during his ministry doesn't seem to be true either. It appears he was very much older. His forty day fast seems to have been undertaken in his early adult years.

To the man sick with palsy,
'Son be of good cheer, thy sins be forgiven thee'

Or to another adult who sought him,

> 'Daughter, be of good comfort thy
> faith hath made thee whole.'

A man in his early thirties, whatever his station would not speak like this to adults. But most indicative of all is the disbelieving question,

> 'Then said the Jews unto him, Thou art not yet
> fifty years old, and hast thou seen Abraham?'
>
> John 9 : 57

To my mind that makes him either forty eight or forty nine at the time.

Before making the above statement 'Daughter be of good comfort, thy faith hath made thee whole' and from within the scrummage that surrounded him, Jesus was heard to ask, 'Who touched me?'

It's likely we imagine a tugging of his clothes or a tap on his shoulder. An individual touch he felt more than all the other touches in the pushing and shoving, for everywhere he went crowds gathered around him.

Jesus instantly knew of one in the immediate vicinity who inwardly loved him dearly, even though she wasn't in view.

What an unforgettable and indelible moment it must have been for that ailing woman. In her own mind she had knelt before him and kissed the hand of his blessed spirit. She had touched his holy consciousness and harmonised with its deep and abiding love. Could there be any more tender touch.

A contemporary nugget of scholarship informs us that the historical Jesus was not a factual person but an Allegory of Wisdom. Whether or not there is any value in isolating the one from the other is not really important anyway, for no one road is right and the other but husk and emptiness.

The essence and vitality of the Christ consciousness, that mysterious influx that is visioned through the heart but inadequately related through the head, remains for all eternity. And as such it does seem an inevitability that this consciousness would at some stage in human history have substantive expression, maybe many times, through form and matter, to continue and intensify the latent and unseen press of the longing for inner awakening, understanding and unity.

Whether the Jesus of scripture is of actual fact, an Allegory of Wisdom or a mix of both, let us take which best suits our particular step, for we will anyway be carried to the same end – our true spiritual core.

Having generally been drawn in life toward the spatial, my personal road since childhood has been the factual, that is, the Christ consciousness revealed through the man Jesus, in flesh and in time. It could just as easily have been the allegorical, for as expressed in these pages, allegory can be enlightening and uplifting in its conveyance of the truth and reality of the holy indwelling consciousness.

The individual can readily appreciate the panoply of allegory, a baptism that leads us onto a pathway to realising our spiritual heritage, a crucifixion as the dieing or dissolution of egocentricity and a resurrection as rebirth into that knowledge of spiritual identity and kinship with Cosmic Consciousness.

A wonder story in itself, but let's not throw the baby out with the bath water by denying the factuality of scripture in its entirety. Symbol and metaphor will have been intimately understood anyway, by those who have the maturity or non-literal temperament to do so.

Not all, with finger pointing precision, follow scripture word by word to find literal interpretation, but find the factual events inspiring and rewarding.

'Walk on' encourages the evangelist. And which-ever road we choose let us shake hands in good blessing at the beginning of our adventure, as we bid each other farewell for a time.

For those not so long in tooth, who may not know of the fact that in days past, when hot water was not so plentiful, children took their turn to bathe in the same bath water. The baby, who was less likely to complain, was always the last into the, shall we say, soapy liquid, hence the ditty.

It is also written that Jesus the man never existed, as no historian of antiquity has made any reference to his existence. This is untrue. Just two references will be quoted and we'll leave the issue there, as what appears deliberate ignorance is most disturbing of the patience.

From annul XV of Tacitus we read,

> 'called Christians by the people, after the originator whose name was Christos. He suffered the extreme penalty during the reign of Tiberius, at the hands of our procurator, Pontius Pilate.'

A second reference made during the first century by a Jewish soldier and historian, Flavius Josephus (his Roman name) and authenticated by Arabic and Syriac works of the ninth and tenth centuries, unearthed by a Mr. Shiomo Pines.

> 'And there arose about this time, Jesus, a wise man. He was the performer of astonishing deeds, a teacher of those who were happy to receive the truth. He won over many Jews and also Greeks .'

Even with the above evidences, according to Mr. C. R. Stewart, in his book 'The Divine Vision,' it is irrefutable that Jesus the Christ was not an historical figure because,

> 'Occult law states that he who has attained superconsciousness is no longer allowed to speak publicly for obvious reasons.'

It is presumed that means, the mob would slay him, or maybe even the governing powers of the day. Although the word 'allowed' in the above statement could do with some expansion, attention must here be drawn to the word 'attained' which itself holds many a key. The child does not attain, it but lives its sublime moments in great natural humility.

We only 'attain' through determination and aggressive self-will. The receptive unspoiled child has no such impediment, so it seems that the statement itself is either guesswork or just another repeated dogma. Either way the statement is at best, flawed.

It appears Mr. Stewart's main objection which compels him to hold such opinion, is the culture of magnifying the person while ignoring the message. In itself of course, a commendable observation and an understandable grievance.

Care must always be taken that we don't allow rules themselves to become our prayer mat and counsel.

In a short appendix Mr. Stewart does confirm however, that,

> 'He who seeks 'self-development' becomes
> a rebel against the Divine Will.'

This brief appendix then becomes more important than the whole preceding narrative, if we ignore the vituperation of those who have attained to cult status.

Also, it is naïve to link or to believe that because there may be a common ancestry of astronomical symbolism in some if not all major religions, that the Rabbi Jesus did not exist. In further attempt to make the birth and ministry of Jesus Christ unimportant, it has been stated that the blessed truths of scripture existed before the birth of Jesus, and were everywhere propagated by pious men in the pre-Christian era.

Astronomical symbolism, (the winter solstice being

a typical example) or pre-existing perennial truths within a community, do not of themselves preclude the existence of Jesus Christ, or the value of those truths he reiterated. In all recorded history there hasn't been a more revelatory personification of the living, active holy indwelling presence. Jesus never claimed to be its inventor, but an instrument through which it gave expression of itself.

To continuously contemplate the man Jesus, the Rabbi Jesus nailed to a timber cross in his final hours, could be considered in some ways, a limiting contemplation, much as the loving widow at the conclusion of her husband's funeral,

"I hate to think of him in that cold ground"

to which her son quietly replied,

"Mother, he isn't there."

While the body of Jesus was being brutalised in crucifixion, the Christ consciousness summoned John to the Mount of Olives, explaining to John that those at the sight of the crucifixion were only aware of what was happening to the body of the Rabbi. Yet, here, bathed in light, the Christ gave much counsel to John, after which John returned to Jerusalem in gladdened heart, for it was only now, that he knew the truth of the living consciousness of the Christ.

That we have statement and parable before us, directly relating to the vast inner consciousness. This that has no form, this that has no selfhood. This that cannot be encapsulated by earthbound minds. This that 'bloweth where it listeth.'

That we have these scriptural statements of the inner consciousness is the greatest gift any generation could bestow upon its progeny. It is the bringing forth of these age-old perennial truths by whatever means, the spirit of Christian scripture being but one, that is most important in our lives.

To listen to the loud babble of commerce, it appears few would agree, but that is only seemingly so, if we are foolish enough to give ear to the rowdy and banal garrulity of the broadcast marketplace.

The statement 'For the flesh lusteth against the Spirit and the Spirit against the flesh' is not how many these days would describe things, but the sense is unmistakable, the contrasting duality of Homo sapiens.

Further, from the Book of Luke, Ch.12, we read,

> 'Suppose ye that I am come to give peace on earth. I tell you, Nay, but rather division.'

There can be no ambiguity about that statement either, but division of what, we may well ask. The conscious division of the spiritual and the carnal? Of course. The increasing awareness of that which is indwelling creates the division within us, often leading to dispute with those of earthbound opinion.

It does seem on the surface to be desperately destructive. What is the purpose of the Christ in Jesus introducing division into the human psyche. Haven't we been led to believe he was a man of peace and don't we have enough problems anyway.

The recognition, however troublesome, of that which lies within – the Christ consciousness, and its relationship to the Highest Principle of Mind, was the continuous demand of the Rabbi Jesus, not necessarily to avoid decadence, neurosis or ignominy, but to bring about a defining contrast in man and in so doing generate a species 'press,' a species need.

The press of both saint and penitent, the press of the forgiving heart and awakening compassion, the press of personal sacrifice made in sanctuary, amphitheatre, prison house and battlefield, on cross or stake.

Without this contrast, division, and resultant species press, the sublime inner consciousness portrayed vividly in scripture and other literature, would not have been 'called' forth into embodiment.

On the one hand we receive the love and succour of the Christ consciousness and on the other, acknowledge the duality within ourselves and in so doing create the press to herald in the Christ consciousness on earth.

A vital indwelling presence attributable to Creative Mind, has capacity and virtue that put it beyond rational conceptions or misconceptions, and that most times is shut out of our lives.

The same man, who in wartime, would risk or sacrifice his own life to comfort or feed an endangered child, would then kill its uniformed father, who had himself but a few years earlier, been that child.

This, a picture illustration of a duality that has the potential to create shocking schisms within us. To be born into human form is to inherit this duality, this potential, and none escape whether that potential becomes apparent or not.

Within this duality lies the essence of the startling contrast between the conscious 'world of men' and the vast inner consciousness, the conscious world of men and the world of the coming Supplant. None would want the assumed, cribbed conscious confinement of the early upright homonid, and none, knowing the choice, would want the conscious confinement of the primate, Homo sapiens.

Birth itself in giving rise to the sentient consciousness creates the duality within us, often unperceived, yet that duality will always remain.

The unimaginableness of the early Christian, and the spirituality of orthodox scripture, – the untapped and often unseen aspect of an inner likeness, to be fully expressed and made manifest in the coming Supplant.

Why, we may ask, would an omniscient Cosmic Consciousness not produce the end result in the beginning. Why go through this process of creation, aeon upon aeon, one step it appears on top of another. Function and process do seem the indomitable twins of material creation, as are space and time. Why they exist at all, may or may not be a problem to us, but to our five sense consciousness exist they do.

An insect may scrutinize the dried ink on this page, but what can it know of the content of word, sentence or paragraph.

To convey and contrast the inner holy consciousness with the shallow lower selfhood, of grasping, ambition and unconscionable dominion is bound to lead to hostility, not only from those of convention and tradition but also from those in power with wealth and privilege (the priesthood in biblical days). In defence of their status, did not the chief priests of the Israelites, state, 'we have no king but Caesar.'

Faced everywhere with the enormity of deceit and self-interest, the Christ would plead in exasperation,

'How much longer must I be with you?'

The inflexible conformity of the world of men can also be seen, when, on the Jewish Sabbath, a certain penniless bedridden cripple of some thirty eight years, is told by this extraordinary holy man, to,

'Rise, take up thy bed and walk.'

The cripple was of a sudden made whole, picked up his bed and after giving thanks and veneration, walked away. The people glorified in what they had witnessed, yet the miracle produced no eye-popping awe in the calcified mindset of the scribes (experts in the written law), for they were, it is said, blind in their own way.

To this profound event, these same scribes displayed no reverence, instead teeth were bared, for the confounded man was breaking the law, he was carrying his bed on the Sabbath.

Wisdom is not knowledge alone, but also knowing how and when to share it.

To the Roman centurion who sought his presence to heal a sick and tormented servant, Jesus said,

'I have not found so great a faith, no not even in Israel.'

We can readily see why Jewish traditional attitude is dismissive, for even those who love their praying to be seen of men, are criticised for their show. It is the closet he advises.

Very often we hold the inner consciousness at arms length or put another way, we keep the door to our prison house – shut. It so longs to give of its wisdom, its light, love and tenderness. It doesn't stand aloof, it doesn't stand aside, we slam the door in its face.

An unswerving friend indeed, yet paradoxically we have to be prepared to open that door, to step out, let go, and face the awesome unfathomable vastness, alone and naked, without defence, trusting implicitly.

> 'Let him be increasingly aware of the Great Void. He whose mind is absorbed there for just a moment, is revered in all worlds. All his store of sin is instantly destroyed. He who has seen it, will never again return to the path of this mortal universe.'
>
> **UPANISHAD**

The heart may tremble or delight in such a promise, yet this seeming shy friend waits patiently, oh so patiently, aeon upon aeon, for it knows its day of joy with us will come, when we take its gentle hand and embrace the embrace of the forever. "Where have you been?" it will whisper in loving greeting. No, never lost, nor estranged, yet forgotten. We have forgotten the higher things of which we were made. The Christ came to remind us.

Such it seems, confirmed by the slave ship captain, who in deep remorse for what he had done, wrote that most beautiful hymn – Amazing Grace.

The inner connsciousness knows all to well our ignorance. The more open we hold the door the greater its revealing presence, and the more distanced we then become to the ways of men (the world).

Either we live the ways of men and remain forgetful of who we are, or we live life more and more in sympathy with this inner consciousness, and become more detached from the ways of the world, introducing division where none existed before.

In our habitual psychology of 'looking out' we see the handiwork of the Universal Consciousness, without. It is through the Christ consciousness within, that the Divine surveys its own creation.

"I am Jesus the Christ, who are you?"
asks the Christ consciousness. How do we answer? I am Mike or I am Jane or I am an accountant, student or shopkeeper. If we did but know, then we could say,
"I am thy brother."
or to nun Maria Vela – "I am thy spouse."

So here we have this revered Prophet of Christendom expressing and revealing in flesh, the inner consciousness, the true heart of man. The Rabbi, the harbinger of the coming species, the divine spirit and consciousness manifesting in sentient form. He is making revelation of the indwelling presence, an expression of its oneness with all creation, and of that which lies within each and everyone of us.

From prehistory and more obviously the last two thousand years of scripture, the vast inner consciousness revealed and expressed by Jesus Christ, and by others of course, has been knocking on every door in every land. Those ripened and ready have responded by opening that door for love, awe, wonder and beauty to enter their hearts and minds. They have been the pioneers, the press, and maybe we don't always appreciate the selfless lives and holy goodwill that these men and women have had for us all, even if confined in cloistered buildings.

With such genuine love and tenderness entering the human heart, it does make the sentiments of Professor Richard Dawkins extremely difficult to understand and to some degree disturbing, when he expresses grief at the seeming impossibility of destroying the 'religious impulse' in man. I'm not sure whether it's the extra-ordinary religious experiences themselves that create such reaction, or the manner in which a whole pyramid of earthly power is built upon them.

The religious impulse in man and the lust to power are two totally different things. There is nothing to fear from he of the religious impulse. He of the political impulse, using religion as a tool to power, is not quite so benign. It is such an explicit difference to be so readily overlooked, for no individual of spiritual insight could possibly pursue earthly power, it has no attraction for him.

In contrast to Professor Dawkins' disappointments, we read,

> 'If all whoever partook of the sacrament had really commemorated the sufferings of Jesus and drunk of his cup, they would have revolutionised this world.'
>
> Mary Baker Eddy

Also, from the lovely sutras of Patanjali we read,

> 'Non-violence in its dynamic condition
> means conscious suffering.'

It is the lot of many men and women to suffer prolonged pain or atrocity. The Christian cross is not only the symbol of the willing suffering of the Rabbi Jesus but also an historic symbol of the potential purity and compassion slain minute by minute in our daily lives.

Maybe the greatest philosophy in human history, because it is most potent and immediate, has been this invite to a moment by moment conscious and deliberate will to partake of mindful non-retribution, and the acceptance of the ensuing pain, especially intense at the beginning of the process.

This moment by moment mindfulness becomes paramount in the effort not to allow ourselves relief in retribution, from the pangs and pains that attend such an adventure. It is such adventures that have led us directly to the Supplant.

One could spend a lifetime in diligent attempts at understanding the head and heart of the religious message. Yet, it is when courage and will are taken in hand and the above instruction followed, even through failure after failure, that things really do begin to come alive. Meticulous study will no longer seem to be a necessity; the life of each spiritual truth will find an instant inner root, resonance and joy.

How can it be that men have set their hearts against themselves, against the gentle promptings of this awesome inner Voice. It is quite astonishing really that those who determinedly avoid this inner recognition often find themselves, not only as psychological counsellors, where all non-parochial psychology becomes a sickness, but unbelievably find themselves in some cases as spiritual advisors.

From the autobiography of the saintly nun Maria Vela, we read that after two hours of confession her new confessor informed her of his firm conviction, that all she had told him was unimportant and illusion anyway. In the translation by Frances Parkinson Keyes we learn how voices guided Maria Vela through much of her life in the convent at Avila and through the smelting torment that is often the lot of those reaching for that holy ground within. The saintly nun was again soberly informed that these Voices were mere imagination, deception or illusions of the Devil. Yet, to the most exalted words of Maria Vela, the inner resonance can be so intense as to feel to reverberate and echo through the universe itself forever.

It appears that the perverse judgments above, were made by convent authorities with sincerity but do encourage one to ask again. How can such authorities be so unresponsive to a warm, vital inner energy and reality? To some extent it can be expected of the gross and earthy, but of those housed in buildings of elevated endeavour, it is most puzzling.

After the many public levitations of Maria Vela, her

superiors decided that she really was possessed of a devil that would have to be exorcised.

Many at the convent in Avila were witness to these arresting levitations, so it was not just hearsay or the word of one who loved the Christ dearly. It really is difficult to square these and other non-logical events with the contemporary self-absorbed materialism. A materialism so saturating of the buffeted Western mind, itself fed with the puerile and trivial, and served with the illusory progress of commerce and politic.

When depiction in film has an entrepreneur assuring us, that 'greed is healthy' it becomes far easier to understand why such otherworldly events become unbelievable.

As these notable events at Avila cannot fit into atomised science because they are not of it, they have to be denied along with the vast and glorious inner consciousness that gives rise to them.

From the Christ consciousness, revealed and expressed in allegory, parable, the Buddha, Jesus, and others, the great spiritual truths and our abiding heritage were reiterated and propagated. Wherever he went, the open spaces, the market place or synagogue, Jesus would re-enunciate these truths. The great power of these truths is in their direct experience, with the Church ideally pointing the way.

While it is frequently repeated that Rome was converted to Christianity, the subjective teachings of Jesus Christ became part of the play of Roman politics, and such politicking continues to this day.

Further, it appears that many in the Western world have been discouraged from the contemplation of scriptural truths because of the recorded persecutions committed down the years, by a church leadership entrusted with those truths.

It has also been evident that through fear of persecution, through inquisitions, stake, rack and other torture apparatus, the church throughout the ages, has retained corporate control of vast populations. Excommunication alone was often an indirect death sentence, and we need not look back to medieval times, for even late into the twentieth century individual careers were dependent upon church membership.

Which of the Crusades were excommunicated because they refused to share the spoils of a sacked Constantinople with the Papacy. To continue in this age of its weakening influence, the Church has adopted a more conciliatory attitude, less dictatorial, yet of necessity remains institutionalised, hierarchical, and heavily involved in the world's financial institutions.

Nonetheless, should garden, sunset, tree or sacrament be the vestibule for the deep instancy of our relationship to the creator of our being, our living, then that we cannot deny.

We cannot deny a garden for the effort it demands, or the sun as it slowly falls out of sight at the horizon, nor the tree so bare in winter. Neither can we deny the church of any denomination because of the worldliness of its antecedent leaders, for in every generation, convents and monasteries have housed, expressed through their human form, the angelic inner nature that resides within each of us.

Scripture contains beautiful truths, especially when they spring to life in the heart, the human custodians of that scripture, throughout history, more than fallible, sometimes brutal. That is how it has been. Truths, often in the hands of those without conscience, regaled in wig and robe, an elite.

We see this elitism consolidated and amplified in a law enacted by the Church of the early fifteenth century. An enactment to deny direct access of the populace to scripture and the words of the Christ. Namely, the decree that any found reading the scriptures in the mother tongue would be dispossessed and put to death. It is even said that Sir Thomas Moore personally whipped those responsible for the printing and distribution of the English version of the Bible.

The Latin version, the Vulgate, isolated in the Church itself, was only understood by those who could read Latin, and that didn't include the peasantry. The spread of the written word in the common language would it was obvious, seriously erode the mystique of the ecclesiastic, and thereby the elite position of those within it. And that is what has happened.

The defence, that the above law was enacted to protect the purity of the written word, we can be sure, was fervently believed by the fundamentalists of the time, yet could be described as obsessive for the

Vulgate would still have remained as a study for future scholars. It has been argued that much of the earthly power of the Church lay within this unwillingness to translate the words of the Christ into the vernacular, allowing the status quo to continue unopposed.

Within any man-made church hierarchy, there always seems a tendency to pull religious experience and knowledge into a centralised power structure. The need of those who seek power or position within the bastions of a church organisation does at times appear to be more urgent than the recognition of the holy indwelling presence itself.

The dispersion of power, of course, is always bad politics. Whenever or wherever we have a healthy diversity of faith, we have a weakening of centralised church power.

According to an early formulator of centralised Christianity – Irenaeus, it is not possible to contemplate the spiritual in any other way than through the medium of literalism and orthodoxy, the present creed of the formal Christian Church.

Of the Gnostic 'heretics,' Ireneaus protests,

> '- - - every one of them generates
> something new every day - - -'

To those who find the Gnostic tenet of 'knowing through experience' as life giving, the hair tearing frustrations of the 'book-keeper mentality' is quite funny in its wide-eyed determination to fixate.

The bishop Irenaeus was of a political mind, seeking

the destruction of diversity in faith, and its replacement with a centralisation of 'divine authority,' within a tiered institution.

Instead of the 'knowing through experience' as advocated by the Christ, (look within), we have had belief through consensus.

There is a suspicion that the denigration of Thomas as a doubter, seems to have been a successful political ploy to denunciate this same gnosis propagated at the time by Thomas and his followers. Thomas was fully aware of the spiritual stature of Jesus. Before the crucifixion, Jesus queried his disciples as to whom he was being compared, Thomas replies,

> 'My lips will only let me say,
> thou hast no equal.'

In 325AD, well over a century after the call of Irenaeus for religious uniformity, bishops from around the Roman Empire were summoned to a high level meet by the warrior emperor Constantine. The agenda – to resolve their politically troublesome differences and formulate an 'orthodoxy' they were all agreed upon. The Nicene Creed is what followed. An enforceable creed backed by statute. Was it similar creed that brought Christ to the cross and his disciples to persecution?

The inflexible religious dogmatist will often see mystical experience as contrivance or invention. Dogmatists also seem to possess within themselves a singular striving for an 'authoritative' dogma. The mystic of any shade is often castigated by hostile reaction to anything that may deviate from the formal interpretation of things. The canons of orthodoxy that have dragged the essential truth of the Christ consciousness through all manner of institution, tumult and falsehood. And yet, is it not the clouded and murky river currents that spread spawn far and wide.

From the outlawed pre-Vatican narratives of Thomas, Philip, The Book of Truth, The Magdalene Papers and others, we learn that those early followers, recognising the spiritual consciousness revealed to them through the Rabbi Jesus, were acutely aware of how that vast consciousness, although one in essence, was infinitely diverse in its manifesting. As diverse as the number of those whom it touched.

In love and respect for one another, the diversification of the experience of the Christ in each life must have brought together those early followers in deep veneration. The love of the Christ, the cement binding all experience.

Spontaneous loose-knit gatherings of the like-minded eventually became unacceptable to those of earthly power, who themselves it seems, cannot understand this diversification of the Spirit, but must have everything set in the solid, in alabaster, pillar and stone, where it can be physically seen and touched. An attempt to compress the Christ consciousness into a confinement of earthly making, to be condensed into ritual and formula, and historically enforced by threat, coercion, and murder.

Unfortunately, once the spiritual becomes formalised and institutionalised, it seems to submerge beneath a body politic, which will often coalesce into bigotry and intolerance.

Formulated religion leads to power blocks which will eventually lead to war. Unformulated veneration, of its very nature, can never lead to war, for no man or group of men can ever own, control or incorporate it, for it is much too diverse. A real pain in the neck to those who seek earthly power, and always endeavour to obtain and retain that power through the homogeneity of institution. And in this context it can easily be seen why the unearthed outlawed Nag Hammadi writings and gospels where so momentous and threatening to the Orthodox Church, as they were in those very early days, and why again, attempts were made to suppress them.

Although church hymn and psalm can be most inspiring, throughout these writings runs a basic encouragement to draw away from the blind acceptance that priest or parson are necessary intermediaries between ourselves and the Transcendental. In the boundless Christ consciousness there are no sectarian interests, denominations or hierarchies.

> What I know of the divine sciences and Holy scripture, I learnt in woods and fields. I have had no other masters than the beeches and the oaks.
> (translator unknown) Saint Bernard

We ourselves must walk on, and not be so indolent as to expect others to do our walking for us, whatever creed they profess.

The canonical church often appears to usurp the Spirit unto themselves or attempt to convince the laity of the church's intercessory omnipotence. Nonetheless the cross remains a symbol of the limitless universal love and compassion, and its never ending potential to 'move through' or 'come unto' us.

These are the most intimate moments we will ever experience and these most precious moments need no earthly organisation or arbiter to incant on our behalf. A natural yet unremitting need and our offering up or self-releasing is the primary necessity, along with an outstretched inner hand.

> 'bread which cometh down from heaven,
> that a man may eat thereof and not die.'
> Jesus the Christ

That bread, that spirit, that inner consciousness Jesus metaphorically describes as his flesh, to drink of his blood, to accept into the fabric of our being the love, life, truth and wisdom of the holy inner consciousness.

Including the disciples and to the great puzzlement of all around to this 'body eating,' Jesus explained,

> 'the words that I speak unto you,
> they are spirit and they are life.'

> 'Give us this day our daily bread'

He who lives only at the physical level will see the word 'bread,' only as the loaf on the table.

We have in the New Testament reference to Jesus Christ as 'Son of Man.' Jesus the Christ knowing himself to be of the Divine,

'The Father and I are one.'

is hardly likely to refer to himself as a son of the Homo sapiens. It is inconceivable he would refer to himself as the son of any species, for the Christ consciousness is not of the body, not of matter, not of species.

Jesus was fully aware of his true identity (his spiritual Self and consciousness) and he would not have locked that identity in with any physical form. In fact, from the outlawed gospels of those who walked with him, hidden at Nag Hammadi about 350AD and found in 1945, we read in the Secret Book of James the words of Jesus,

'be ye like the Son of the Holy Spirit.'

While the Hebrew term 'Ben-Adam' is mostly interpreted as Son of Adam or Son of Man, some Jewish scholars have made the point that the Hebrew word 'dam' means blood.

We see this 'blood' is not the body blood of the Rabbi Jesus but a symbolic or metaphorical reference to the Holy Spirit he expresses. Therefore the term Ben-Adam, is more fittingly translated as,

'Son of the Holy Spirit.'

A transcendental, non-literal interpretation which makes sense.

So, it would definitely appear that the phrase 'Son of Man' has a metaphorical meaning, with Man as the crucible. The Son, as an heir, written with a capital letter suggests a special heir. That Son being the indwelling Christ consciousness. What more wonderful revelation could there be. That each of us, equally, have this Heir within us, has always been the best news ever given to humankind. We can readily see how such good news has been spread to every part of the planet. And it is not a matter of belief, it is a matter of knowing or not knowing.

We don't become more spiritual, we are of an inner spirit, a holy inner consciousness, an indwelling spirituality. Wafer and wine in themselves are potent symbols of that spirit and life; spirit and life that we are instructed to ponder in closet and in prayer, but as Jesus says, he speaks of spirit, not of the body. The need to understand symbol and metaphor.

The ministrations of Jesus are of a subjective nature directed at the very heart and mind of the individual, and were certainly, never meant to be used as a tool to power.

A hierarchical structure of earthly authority may be ideal when forcibly welding a population together in communal effort, but it has nothing to do with the Christ consciousness or the ministrations of Jesus.

To those on the 'contemplative ray,' this longing or lust for earthly power appears a madness, a lifelong madness, for without the will to wound or kill, this earthly power is unobtainable. In other words, those who yearn for power must have the will to kill, if not directly, then by proxy, if they are to obtain and retain that power.

That this will to kill does prevail today is more than obvious. That it exists in the corridors of the body politic, and even commerce is self-evident and part of biological motivation. That it has existed within Vatican walls, is further exposed, in detail, within the pages of David Yallop's work 'In Gods Name.' An explicit exposure of the Machiavellian murder of the goodly Pope, Albino Luciani in 1978. The papal figure-head who sought to reduce the preoccupation of the Vatican with its financial advisors, and the inevitable involvement with visible corruption. As is often repeated here, the drive to dominion by whatever means is of the earthly, of the Homo sapiens.

And as regards to the assumption of the future projected longevity of the institutional Church in all its form, the Church is most certainly mistaken, for nowhere in the coming commune of the Supplant can there be any such genetically inherited desire for hierarchy or dominion.

Dominion is no part of the inner consciousness, no part of the Christ, and therefore no part of the coming Supplant.

CHAPTER SIX

THE CHRIST IN JESUS

> 'There is no more noble employment of a man's time than to ponder the works of the Creator.'
>
> Gotama the Buddha

Any social shortcomings or unhappiness within Western cultures, as commented upon by clinical psychologist Mr. Carl Yung, are but a small problem, a festering boil compared to the heavy body of destructive atheism so prevalent in both the erudite and the ignorant within those cultures.

Atheism has its own power of conviction, and becomes the only way the lower carnal self can remain free from the unsettling selfconscious duality, free from the knowing of division, and free from the ideation and turmoil that initially spring into both head and heart.

The comfortable world of the purely logical and cognitive must of necessity be rent asunder. Revelation or realisation never seem to appear without rupture. Until the seed case splits no flower will bloom, no apple tree mature, no fruit will ripen. So it appears to be with the encased mind of the rational.

Could the holy inner consciousness have produced the amphitheatres of Rome, the Crusades, the thumbscrew, the Church terror of the Middle Ages, the callous and heartless abduction, shipping and enslavement of some twelve million indigenous people from their African homeland, the corrosive doctrine of hell-fire and damnation, the bestial concentration camps, the infanticide of convenience abortion and the blessing of weapons of war, all in its own name.

It has also been stated that the influence of Christianity in the West has been ineffective in eliminating warfare. Why should we expect the words and purity of a single expression of the Christ consciousness on earth, to rid the Homo sapiens of war.

The combative nature of the species is continued through its blueprint type reproduction, and also through that bastion of its organisation, the pyramid of power. Without hierarchy there can be no power. Without power there can be no war. Of the civil, only persuasion is an option, for the word civil itself of course, means non-military.

That wars would continue ad infinitum with the breeding Homo sapiens was all too obvious to the Christ, as was the continuing division within successive generations, as men were drawn inwards, towards the inner consciousness, until the press be so great, man the creature, the biological creature, through dissatisfaction with its own earthbound selfhood would have willed its own extinction, and in so doing, allow a greater conscious and spiritual breadth to prevail.

Not a heaven, in some imagined region of the sky or outer space for a privileged few, but a heaven right here on this beautiful planet, its verdant rolling hills, its dense forests, its solitary deserts and endless plains, its cloud flecked skies, warm breezes and heaving blue seas. Its scented flowers and swaying trees, its myriad life forms.

It has been wondered why Jesus schooled and preached at all, of our indwelling spirituality and its divine relationship to Cosmic Consciousness, when he knew perfectly well that the church of men to follow would be the church of men that schemed his death and would still be of unmerciful dominion, and brutal to many folk of integrity, probity and veneration.

The seeds were being sown. In our spatial world of opposites, relativity and linear time, we see but narrowly. In new speak, the big picture escapes us. The Rabbi Jesus saw the intense 'press' to come from his re-revealing of the vast and not of this world, inner consciousness, to the often reluctant attention of the earthbound, eventually to instigate and to issue forth the new species. A species manifesting and expressing on earth, the Christ consciousness.

So great a thing to die for, he saw the division he would create, he saw the eventual press within the heart of man and the longing to be relieved of the lowly status. A most noble yearning, also within the heart of man, is this wish to forsake its own condition. He saw the battle to be played out within the species. 'I bring a sword not peace.' He saw the coming of the new species form, the Supplant – the second coming.

It is not to an improvement of culture or social conditions that we look. It is not to refinement of the species either, even though the peacemakers be of good intent and most try to control baser instincts.

With the expectation of a Messiah of armour and might to send the Romans packing, the Jewish populace were mistaken the first time around.

With the expectation of an individual coming to save the world of men from themselves, the Gentiles are mistaken this the second time around.

The second coming is not a personage to again be butchered and brutalised by the robed and the uniformed, but the unimaginable inner presence and consciousness along with its sublime love and compassion, expressed in species and bodily form, made manifest in the flesh.

The hierarchical that feeds, clothes and houses many an unfortunate, may be the very best we can presently produce and the result of the goodness of many men and women. Nonetheless as commendable as it is, it is of the human, necessary to the human as is the hierarchical structure of a military defence, but it is of the human. The continuation of the species Homo sapiens is the continuation of its circumstance and inherent duality. The creature is the creature and can only perpetuate that creature. That which is of the Supplant is something entirely different.

'My God, my God why hast thou forsaken me?'

This supposed utterance of Jesus when hanging from

the cross was always a mystery, especially when we are informed in the next verse that onlookers asked if he was calling for Elias, who would not have been considered his God, but more likely a friend in brotherhood.

How can the immanent holy presence, the Christ in Jesus, the Supplant to come, make question of being forsaken by that which it is. Having no knowledge of Hebrew or Aramaic, a puzzle it had to remain.

After much research and travel, Mr. H. Spencer Lewis has claimed that the original script reads, 'Heoli, Heoli,' and not 'Eloi, Eloi.' The translation of 'Heoli, Heoli,' approximating to, 'My bothers, My brothers,' making sense of the comment concerning Elias. The complete line reading,

> 'My brothers, my brothers, why
> hast thou forsaken me?'

Is Jesus asking why his brethren or disciples have fled? This is hardly likely for he knew that would happen long before he picked up the weighty cross.

So if it wasn't the man consciousness speaking, then it was the holy consciousness speaking through the man, through the Rabbi Jesus. A holy man of such profound wisdom, love and compassion being put to death by his own people. What an obscenity. Yet in this act of such profane ingloriousness we hear him asking each and everyone of us why we have abandoned the ME of the Cosmic.

The use of the word 'brothers' drawing us unto him and further cleaving the division. The Cosmic Consciousness, the scriptural Heavenly Father is asking through the dying Jesus,

> 'My people of Earth, why have you forsaken Me, why have you shut out my presence until you no longer even recognise Me when I am before you in the flesh and beside you in the Spirit. As has always been my wish, let Me be in you and you in Me.'

More explicit and profound than ever expressed before, with the coming of the Christ in Jesus this devastating seed is sown into the human psyche, an injection of such ideation. So much so, that man as a species would be destined never again to be at peace with itself.

The sword honed, the war in the mind begun, the conscience called forth and ignorance caught in the spotlight of its own narrow nature.

With the coming of conscience, the will to goodness is strengthened yet the dislocation that follows the inner recognition or awareness produces great uncertainty, for with this recognition of the split, the pull from one to the other, tensions and stresses are unavoidable.

An objective, possibly the main objective, of the Christ in Jesus was to wean men away from the potentially barbarous lower self, and with increasing awareness of the inner consciousness, create the species press deep within the human collective and thereby further promote the species change and the eventual coming forth of the inner consciousness unencumbered by ego, yet fully revealed in biological form. (Thy kingdom come. Thy will be done on earth as it is in heaven.)

Man has been faced with the horns of a dilemma, either cowardly remain free of the troublesome division, and retain, undisturbed, a narrow yet dominant rationalism, or, recognise the innate limitations of the earthbound concrete mind, however wizard or clever, and accept the ensuing difficulties to come.

Difficulties that lead directly to the progressive realisation of the enormous potential and wonder of that which is indwelling, and eventually to the longing to live as that, and only that.

What greater 'press' to renewal could there be, for is not 'evolution,' expressed as divine creation, precisely that – renewal. Symbolically, we are going home.

'The land that is nowhere, that is our true home.'

Yu Ching

And presently, to those, who in incarnation, mourn the loss of their spiritual home, it is they as well, who shall be comforted.

Yet that home is to have its fulfilment on planet earth where life will be lived entirely as the unbounded and timeless indwelling presence. No personal ambition, as we know it, will exist, or could possibly exist, for the thought of the one will be known of the whole.

A consciousness of such depth and breadth, as to be unimaginable to us at the present moment even though we may at times, have been but touched by it, and that, sufficient to create an overpowering need for its further expression, not only in ourselves but in each and everyone.

It must be repeated that these commentaries are herein written as I have come to understand, and are not based on youthful ideal or the quixotic.

This awesome inner consciousness, in its elemental purity is not able to fully or permanently express through the human form, no more than vocabulary or the abstract can fully or permanently express through the chimpanzee, the gorilla or any other animal. They don't have the organic form.

So it will be, the interminable struggle and restlessness in the heart of man will be at an end. Conflict, being no part of the Supplant, will pass from the earth. Now we can speak of transmutation, for here begins the end of a species and we shouldn't be surprised that some, in their intensity, will feel the overpowering need to resist. A resistance not only evident in many an individual but equally evident in various parts of the human collective.

Despised and rejected of men, of course there will always be hostile, if not brutal reaction within the species, to the initiator, the harbinger, and also to the immanent extinction of the species itself, however elevated or magnificent the forthcoming incarnating succession may be.

The opposing desire to normalise, not to bring to the highest common denominator, will always seek to transform the most eminent into ordinariness.

We should remember, Jesus was acknowledged as wiser and more knowing than any, even when still in infancy. This is hardly open to question, for even on a superficial level we have seen the young, able to square, random multidigit numbers instantaneously, which means there is a static point where all that has been and will be, is known.

And was it not said of him,

'How knoweth this man letters, having never learned?'

The inner consciousness is not bounded by the patterns of cognitive conceptual thought and is certainly not bound by scientific parameters.

CHAPTER SEVEN

A QUESTION OF SCIENCE

We presently don't appear to be aware of the then desperate and insatiable need of the post renaissance intellect to construction and invention. From perpetual motion, electricity, mechanisation and the power of steam, to the constructs of theory in the advancing sciences of biology and psychology.

The God of scripture and laity becomes the 'group mind' which man must serve because he is 'spiritually created by the group mind.' Such was the contentious need of a communal intelligentsia rebounding from hundreds of years of despotic, ecclesiastic and cultural oppression. An understandable reaction in many ways, but somewhat distorted when that 'group mind' is claimed to be divine and the aggressive atheism defended as 'not being in a spirit of wanton hostility.'

That is precisely the ground in which many of the nineteenth and twentieth century plausible theories were fashioned and rooted. Ironically by attempting to deflect the truth of motive, that motive has unwittingly been revealed.

A continental intellect suddenly released from the incarcerating grip of the tyrants of Mighty Church, is bound to want to emasculate the organisation and of course everything it stood for.

It must be a serious consideration that the main reason for the formulation and acceptance of the Darwinian theory of evolution for example, has been an emotional need to be released from the obligation, supervision and authority of Church inculcation, its earthly power and unfortunately the inevitable denial of everything transcendental.

By attempting to relieve the hierarchical church of its power, through the forces of a released and bludgeoning intellect, the wonder of the inner consciousness has in many respects been crushed in the process. It's like poisoning all the fish in the seas to kill off the dreaded sharks, and thereby leaving ourselves hungry.

Mr. Darwin, although the son of a church minister was obviously more influenced by the thrusting arrogance of a 'faith in human progress' and the proposed coming development, through science, of the 'ideal man.' Mr. Herbert Spencer was certain that the birth of this 'ideal man' was inevitable, again he was right, but not as expected through the hand of man.

These eighteenth and nineteenth century humanists were deluded in their conviction that 'Man is the master of all things.' An egotism unctuous in its pride maybe, yet significantly we can also see the desire and yearning for an end to human suffering and unhappiness, and the longing to herald in an era of goodwill among all men.

As the God of scripture had not provided these paradisiacal conditions in the previous two thousand years, then with the bursting forth of a latent hubris man was going to do it himself.

This impatience is mentioned here only to show that although the will be misplaced the intention was noble indeed and again part of the inner press and longing, even in its apparent ungodliness.

Because the species to come – The Supplant, is of new form, and substantially different from its predecessor the Homo sapiens, it is at this point we must look more closely at the Darwinian theory of evolution that has become culturally institutionalised as if of fact.

The contemporary scientist tells us that the foundation of Darwinian theory is based upon a possibility that mutation, chance and accident, (aimless creation) can lead to advantageous genetic alteration, retained through the survival of those progeny most fitted to exist in the prevailing environment (natural selection). With one creature becoming another through slow sequential mutated change over aeons of time.

Mr. Darwin, in his work 'On the Origin of Species,' uses the word 'variation' to explain the differences in form within species, both useful and non-useful. The two words now generally used to explain these differences are variation and mutation. For the purposes of these writings, variation is taken to convey the inherent healthy use by the organism of innate differentiation, or the diversity of form springing from within the circumscribed yet complete package of genetic information that the animal inherits from its parents – the genome.

Mutation, on the other hand, is taken to mean an occasional **UNHEALTHY** aberration within the genome. A gene misconstruction outside the species genetic boundary. A variation will survive, whereas a mutation will not, for mutation is always injurious to the organism in which it resides, be that organism a mammoth or a microbe.

Also, to avoid too much ambiguity, the word species in this narrative is taken to mean similar form that reproduce similar fertile offspring. Genus is taken to mean families of species that may not be able, within themselves, to produce fertile offspring. For example, tiger, lynx, panther, lion, or wolf, fox, dingo, or horse, donkey and zebra, or eagle, owl, raven and wren.

The question is not so much whether the specifics of a species or genus appear through accident, design or universal law, but whether the potential variation itself appears through accident, design or an as yet, unknown universal law; for without the span of variation, the beauty and wonders of complex form would not be so diverse.

Because we may see a possible biological relationship between the hand of man, the paw of the mole and the fin of the dolphin, it does not follow that each new genus, or species, is the product of chance, accident or mutated creation, whether such creation be instant or gradual. And then, the same all the way back to the first trilobite?

Even if these similarities were biologically related, it is still but hypothesis, that time, accident, mutation and chance could have brought this about.

Mutation, accident and chance can lead anywhere, they are blind, without vision or function, without aim or potential, certainly a cohesive potential, for everywhere we look in nature we see the ordered formation of life, an ordered creation. Darwinian evolutionists deny this and insist that all creation is random.

In the world of flora and fauna because a degree of variation within each family of species (genus) has been observed, it again doesn't follow that this variation leads to the origin of new genera. If variation is confined to a predetermined and inherent limitation, which is bound within the relevant genome; then genus origination, as a result of variation, is not possible.

While the simple organism, the nematode, we are informed, has no variation which means each organism is identical, it does appear in general that one of the tools of survival in the armoury of species is this combination of potential and manifest variation. An inbuilt genetic feature from inception.

Where variation is self-evident, biological pairing will produce genetic variation in each offspring. Human to human the variation is about 0.1%, a huge proportion in DNA terms, which means of course, no two individuals can be identical. Yet, the species remains bound within the variation box, for the entirety of its existence on earth. In other words, a trammelled lineage from which no other genus or family of animal can possibly emerge by way of this proffered slow linear evolution.

The wide variety of show dog are all bred from the wolf, and are all born within the box of variation of the canine genome. Man has exploited that potential variation and from it, developed the Pekinese, the Afghan Hound and everything in between, yet we still have a dog type and not a slug, rabbit, rat or daffodil.

We would clearly see natural selection (or common sense) in action, were these animals to be returned to the wild. Only those fitted to survive would survive.

Where ranging and stamina are a necessity, those of stumpy legs would be gone, those of flattened face and short breath would be gone, as would those with no fur and unable to survive one night outside. The death of the dogs, ill-bred from the genome, to survive back in the wild as it presently exists.

If the environment remained unchanged, it is inevitable that the surviving dogs would be of variation closest to the wild dog shape, once man was out of the equation. Yet all these variations of dog produced by man would still exist in potential and within the boundaries of variation of the surviving canine genome.

Man hasn't 'made' the Pekinese or the Doberman or the Black Labrador, he has but exploited a huge potential that was there at inception. The enormous complexity of the dog genome, or any genome, has surely not been 'put there' by chance, accident or mutation.

The scientist informs us that he can take a carefully

selected phosphorescent gene from a jellyfish, stick it in a fox and lo and behold the fox lights up. But how and where in nature is that going to happen. Glowing in the dark, his element of surprise would be gone. He would die of starvation, again culled by natural selection.

Let us say some within the human population survive a plague. Due to species variation those individuals who survive, are, or have become, resistant or immune to the pathogen, so they breed and the plague if it remains unaltered (with little or no variation) will eventually lose its infective power and stagnate or perish through the lack of a vulnerable host.

The inbuilt potential variation within a species gives it a greater probability of survival, if faced with a changing or changed external environment. If an organism or creature hasn't a broad enough variation band within its biological make-up, to survive environmental onslaught then that creature will become extinct. And that appears to be the case for the largest mammal, the smallest insect or wittiest hominid.

Mr. Darwin's 'natural selection' should really be confined to species variation as he indicates. However, the leap that then requires this 'natural selection,' within the variation boundary of a species, to produce a new genus or different type of animal entirely, is a very feeble idea and plainly wrong.

Mr. Darwin also contends that differences in any one species have 'descended.' Species variety, it has otherwise been stated, is an inherent potential within the species genome, and this biological or genetic potential was there at inception, it wasn't afterwards created, it became manifest.

Mr. Darwin does later conclude however,

> 'A large amount of hereditary modification
> is at least possible.'

Hereditary modification equals variation of course.

Some species have quite an extensive potential variation. The primula species of flower (primulaceae) for example, humorously described by one young horticultural commentator as promiscuous. The off-spring of cross pollination, in both colour and form, are often almost unrecognisable, one plant to another, yet are all of variety innate within the species plant genome. Mr. Darwin does confirm the same with the cauliflower, cabbage and sprout. All are derived from a single wild brassica form, themselves can be cross pollinated and again are all of variety innate within the particular species plant genome.

A hybridist of plant or animal will increasingly come to know the limits of variation (gene pool) within which he is working. If the DNA code of instruction is boundaried within the genome, it follows that no off-spring can emerge outside the hard line of that boundary. Hence the need to artificially alter, to splice and re-splice with meticulous precision, the DNA itself. To shift those limits and boundaries to produce a marginally altered species which is seen, either rightly or wrongly, as a 'frankenstein' offspring. And well it may prove to be. We just do not know the long term outcome. One thing is certain however, we have introduced something into the natural world that wasn't there before and because of the inevitable proliferation cannot ever be removed, whatever the outcome.

It may take thousands of hybrid crosses before the plantsman can find a commercially viable offspring, which will itself, if fertile, immediately revert back to one or other of the original parent stock, (usually the dominant) unless of course propagation takes place through a vegetative process.

Further along we have the lordly suggestion by Mr. Darwin, that the interbreeding or hybridising of the extremes in a genus (the horse and donkey) which leads to the infertile mule, is a 'strange arrangement' for any Creator. Surely no more strange than the daily birth of countless billions of weak or imperfect spermatozoa, yet life in all its forms, continues.

Mr. Darwin did also write,

> 'there is no fundamental difference between men and the higher mammals in their mental faculties.'

Faced with the above statement, is one supposed to remain composed and discuss the issue without expletive and with a civil tongue. The faculty to language alone, needs enormous mental power, and to express the abstract in language, or mandala maybe, is way beyond the potential of any jungle primate, even though the chimpanzee for example, may exhibit a primitive, mickey-taking sense of humour or even an elementary selfconsciousness.

From early invertebrates, to reptiles, to mammals, to contemporary Homo sapiens, there does appear to be 'progress.' Latterly, the leap in brain size which could be construed as progress. For, with this increase in brain size comes a greater capacity to intelligence, not necessarily ratiocinative intelligence, but intelligent capacity nonetheless.

According to the fossil record the advent of the bipedal hominoid was of sudden appearance. We are informed it pops into biological history as a fully formed, altogether upright walking and dancing biped. It has five inline non-grasping toes on the end of an arched and rigid foot. Its pelvis is totally different to the ape. It has a shorter pelvis and rounded back plate to accommodate the powerful buttock muscles, allowing smooth vertical locomotion, impossible in the ape or anything else in the animal kingdom.

The fact that an ape is able to raise itself into an ungainly fairly upright position, (especially when shown buoyed up in water) is deemed 'proof' of slow progressive evolution. A smattering of intelligence tells us its nothing of the sort, for so can the reptile, the bear and the meerkat, the feline and many a supple jointed horse or canine.

The spinal cord entry in the early bipedal species of creature is under the skull and not towards the back of the skull as in the jungle primate. Of human shape the palate is arched, and again unlike the ape, the canines are small. The teeth are parabolic in formation whereas in the ape and ape-like creatures they are parallel.

The creature Australopithecus (fossils ranging back three million years) only had a brain size of some 500cc and after much excited acclaim, is now deemed to be of the quadruped ape family and not of the biped species of creature.

The biped Homo erectus had a mean brain size of about 1000cc. The biped Neanderthal had a mean brain size of some 1800cc. The later Homo sapiens having a smaller brain at some 1400cc.

So in contradiction to present linear 'evolutionary' theory we can see that this genealogy is not sequential and does not indicate a 'progressive development of the hominid brain,' as stated by Professor Winston. This history of the brain of the biped indicates distinct and separate creatures, whether of Homo erectus and its cousins, (Java man, Peking man), the Neanderthal or Homo sapiens.

Brain size in primates can, from one species to another, decrease in size as well as increase in size. This also applies to many other mammals and even birds. Again this single one-way-ticket 'development' is just not true.

It is with so much enthusiasm that both materialist and the occasional theologian, snap at the sprat of Darwinian slow mutated evolution, and in the process seem to forget that it is still only a theory, a very shaky theory indeed to many scientists and laymen.

Another example repeated by the slow evolutionist

is that of the flounder. A one time upright fish buried itself on its side in the sand and unsurprisingly found one of its eyes pointing downwards and the other pointing upwards. It then evolved, we are told, by its one eye moving nearly one hundred and eighty degrees to be on top, so they could both now look upwards.

Is there anything to substantiate such a preposterous and asinine notion, say a forty five degree or ninety degree off-set eye in fossil form, or for that matter any intermediate form. Surely, there should be considerable fossil evidence of this roving eye, there is none. It's just another part of the mishmash of vivid imagination and ridiculous speculation, masquerading as intelligent understanding.

In the newborn fry of the flatfish, the eyes are positioned as in ordinary fish, either side of the body but within weeks the eyes have moved into the typical flatfish configuration with both eyes facing upwards.

It is stated, by the learned, that this rapid infant development is evidence of slow progressive evolution. A reflection in speeded up form of a pre-supposed slow aeon-long evolution. A classic 'evolutionary' leap in imagination and of course has no validity in truth, for this early development of the flatfish fry, could just as readily reflect an instant creation.

It is unlikely to be anything other than what our eyes tell us it is – an infantile biological process. To suggest anything else is little more than fragmentary speculation, and as such, again makes for extremely feeble theory. To many a layman, this willy-nilly unsubstantiated guessing just does not fit into what he understands as the empiric sciences of test and proof.

If the DNA or gene shifts postulated in Darwinian theory, are brought about by chance, random mutation and accident, the result can lead anywhere, ungoverned it has no direction. Instead of the eye of the flounder moving to a convenient site on the top of the head, it could equally end up in any position.

An eye that has moved one degree to left or right is still in the sand, as is an eye that has moved one degree down the body. The eye could eventually surface at the tail end, "to hell with it, this can't be right," growls the eye. And all this assumes the other eye doesn't go walkabout, and of course this miracle of mathematical chance had to happen to two fish at exactly the same time, in exactly the same place, otherwise there could be no reproduction.

At this point when the going gets messy, we are patronisingly informed that we are mistaken in that 'evolution' (through chance, accident, mutation) takes place in communal form, not in individual form. This, but another deliberate attempt to obfuscate. Any explosion in the population of a 'new' species still has to have a biological beginning somewhere. Proliferation is then, just an inevitability. The problem of a single point beginning cannot be dismissed that easily.

Anyway, the one eye moving one degree in any direction is still in the sand and ineffective. So are we expected to accept that mutation, chance and accident knew the right direction to take, for any non-flat fish with one eye on its way around the body, and cocked at say twenty degrees, is a non-survivor anyway, it's deformed, as is the thinking that originates such bubblegum nonsense.

Wild speculation and guesswork should be given a cupboard all its own, for to try and disprove something that had no validity in the first place, should be solely restricted to nutty professors in quiet corners of reading rooms. Give them pen and paper, then keep well away.

It may be worthwhile repeating a paragraph attributed to novelist Mr. Jack Williamson, who proposes,

> 'human will married to the forces of the subconscious, can influence genes and molecules to such an extent that evolution to a more advanced level can be initiated.'

Again, while the influence of will and subconscious could be considered as a possible motivating force, it is not my understanding that this internal force or press, can of itself produce form change from one genus to another. The power of variation, isolated to the species or genus genome; with human will, of itself, being much too feeble.

> 'Sudden transformation through an internal force - - - - seems to me to enter the realms of miracle and to leave those of science.'
>
> Mr. Charles Darwin

An 'internal force' (if understood as a species press)

on its own, as a power to species change, one must agree, is highly unlikely. As a propulsive to species change, that's a different proposition altogether, with some sort of unrecognised universal law, aback of a potential instant variation and also aback of the instant birth of new genus.

Fossil evidence does appear to point more directly to the instant creation of species. What instigates that snap of creation we may not know, but that doesn't mean we have to be blind, through fear of where our eyes may lead us.

Even today among the varied scientific disciplines many conclude that each genus (kinds?) and possibly each species, has to have been the subject of instant creation, the instant coherent structuring of a gene base, by whatever means.

For example, fully formed and of sudden appearance is the bat, the only flying mammal. The earliest fossil of a bat ranges back some fifty million years or so, and in rocks older than that there are no bats. The bat, in all its forms, still has a recognisable physiological structure and potential variation. The bat species, the bat genus, has lived, from its inception fifty million years ago, and survived as a bat, even if of variant form, to the present day. On much the same time scale, the common house fly is still the common house fly.

While the truth of sentient creation may be much more complex than we imagine and outside our present orbit of comprehension, we should not be expected to accept this unsupported linear sequential theory as fact.

The enormous reach of geological time is no benefit itself either, in the attempted 'inferential proof' of slow sequential evolution, anymore than say the length of the Nile is to the evolution of the shrimp. It's just another red herring.

To return to 'Darwin's thoroughly marshalled argument' and in particular to this business of mutation. The words mutation and variation are often used as synonymous terms. The word variation, as already stated, is used here, to indicate the healthy use of inherent variation within the organism itself, whereas the word mutation is taken to mean an occasional **UNHEALTHY** abnormality within the gene.

In dramatic contrast to contemporary scientific statute, Mr. Darwin states that all non-beneficial variation *(mutation)* within a species will be eradicated, and in that we have to agree with him, whether we call its death natural selection or just inevitable.

It is becoming more apparent that mutation can never lead to improvement of any species let alone a completely new species and surely not, new genus.

And it must always be remembered that not only is a mutant creature repulsive to its own and therefore has little chance of breeding and continuing that mutation, but is inevitably ostracised or killed by the relevant species group, especially that of the higher jungle primates. Born of normality but of subsequent injury, such survivors may be tolerated at the bottom of the food chain, as the runt will.

It is demonstrable that gene mutation leads only to

loss of vigour and to eventual sterility. All mutations are harmful to the organism which is often doomed to quickly perish. If this were not the case, the species itself, would rapidly decline through mutant degeneration, just as the human body does when beset with mutant malignancy.

Mutation, somewhat rare in nature, cannot be the 'fuel of evolution' as claimed by evolutionists. It could be the inflammable destructive fuel of the present evolutionary theory, but hardly the energy or power source responsible for species differentiation.

Cancer or malignant growth, as mentioned, is a mutation, the mutation of a gene in a cell, which then multiplies to form a mass of aimless tissue. This growth or gene mutation itself, (a spelling mistake in the DNA) is often caused by forces destructive to protoplasm, mainly chemical toxins, viral infection and radiation. Hardly the stuff of a vibrant and vigorous new species.

Without both random mutation and arbitrary blind chance, the two major theoretical contemporary mechanisms for change, slow evolution cannot stand alone, which results in 'natural selection,' in its turn, becoming isolated to variation.

For, whatever part of a species (the luckiest often) survives in the prevailing environment, the potential variation of that species survives within the surviving genome. Only certain bodily variation may be temporarily lost, the blueprint to its possible revival and reproduction remains, untouched, unstained and intact, ready to re-proliferate in future generations, carrying the conglomerate variation onward.

Scientists have marvelled at the enormous breadth of variation that the AIDS/HIV virus possesses. They have seen nothing quite like it before. To say it mutates rather than being a **variant** of its predecessors appears to be loose and ill-chosen terminology, when, as already stated, mutation of itself, can only lead to degeneration of the organism.

As well as genetic immunodeficiency (SCID), cystic fibrosis, haemophilia, Huntington's chorea, and hundreds more illnesses stemming from gene abnormality or mutation, we have another genetic mutation within the human DNA producing sickle cell anaemia. An often fatal blood disorder, to which the malaria parasite is obviously resentful, as it cannot breed in the anaemic or abnormal conditions.

When the disease is described as a genetic advantage, because 'anti-malarial,' it does indicate how desperate Darwinian evolutionists have become.

Mutation is always injurious to the organism, always harmful. Sickle cell anaemia alone, shows the devastation that even a tiny or single point mutation can make to the organism.

The human organism and its depleted red blood cells may be uninviting to the malaria parasite, but of far greater importance is the possibility of passing on the degeneration, the mutation, to successors. Even if not sterile and not proving terminal, the organism has seriously reduced vitality, and probably seriously reduced longevity.

It is again but speculation, and scientifically incorrect, to hold that mutation can at any time lead to a new species or be beneficial to any organism. If the mutation is not immediately eradicated through death or sterility of the host, then degeneration is taking place. There is not one single instance, anywhere to be found, in any science or discipline, of beneficial mutation.

Such are the deleterious effects of mutation on the animal or plant, that organisms have their own internal mechanisms for repair, in effort to remove the offending and unwelcome mutation. The immediate reaction of any organism to mutation, is to eliminate it. It is dangerous and therefore cannot possibly be of benefit.

Both variation and mutation produce an alteration in the DNA sequence or code of instruction. The difficulty often appears to be the recognition of one from the other before maturation.

In order to support the evolutionary theory, the geneticist may use a ratio, of one thousand harmful mutations to one of supposed benefit. Even with such an optimistic ratio as this, the organism and its species are heading for rapid extinction, with no possibility of producing any vital new offspring.

It does increasingly appear that educated men and women have hemmed themselves in, behind a wall of make-believe imagination.

A lecturer of Darwinian evolution, at the conclusion

of his talk was asked by a greengrocer if he could provide just one example of beneficial mutation. Taken by surprise it seemed, his brief answer was no. He immediately looked around before quickly heading for the nearest exit. The greengrocer, in mock urgency, asking if there was a fire somewhere in the building.

Put a white moth in a forest and for survival sake in a few generations, we have been told, the moth through mutation or mutated adaptation will assume the colour, of the tree bark. We are also informed that this is further 'proof' of natural selection and slow graduating evolution.

The above conclusion, arrived at from 'observation' wasn't either mutation or mutated adaptation. Because of the progressive increase in industrial pollution the darker bark became revealed as the lighter coloured lichen, crusted on the trees, withered and fell to the ground. The white mottled moths, becoming easier prey for the local birds, eventually died out.

Both the light and dark moths were physiologically the same. There was obviously no mutated species change. It wasn't in any way adaptation, evolution, mutation or any other imagined development. It was simply the survival of the variation of the moth most suited to the changing or changed environment and that aspect of variation was there at the inception of the moth. No mutation, no species change, no evolution. The dark moths survived, the lighter moths were more easily picked off, leaving few or none to breed.

The above instance is related here, only to show

how typically, the Darwinian preconception first existed in the mind of the observer, the facts were then moulded to fit.

This peppered moth business has been scientifically described as one of the best examples of evolution occurring through natural selection. No 'evolution' has taken place for the black peppered moth was and still is, physiologically, a fully altogether, singing and whistling peppered moth. The 'science' was wrong.

Unless the scientist has greater validity and is more evidenced in his argument, then the distrust, as expressed earlier, can only increase, both within the professions and within the circle of laymen who refuse to be browbeaten with the wet flannels of academia, as the white peppered moth is once again on the increase.

It really must be repeated and underlined, that ALL mutations are injurious to the organism, and that there are no known beneficial results from mutation, in any science or discipline.

This concurs with Mr. Darwin's observation in his 'On the Origin of Species;' to repeat, that all 'non-beneficial variation *(mutation)* will be eradicated.' It therefore appears that the idea of mutation as a motive force in so-called evolution, is but a modern addition to a linear hypothesis, and is no part of Mr. Darwin's theory at all. This recent idea, appears to have been woven into the fabric of the Darwinian theory, not only because of the authority that the word Darwin has amassed unto itself, by a propagating, concept driven intelligentsia, but also because, accident and chance are even more ludicrous as a motive force in the wonders of creation.

With this theory of mutation and chance, genetic accidents and slow sequential evolution coming under continuous denial from many areas of science, comes greater understanding of the self-assertive rebound from the unbridled and strangulating control of the Church of Rome. A power structure formulated for the convenience of Roman emperors, and which, for hundreds of years, through unyielding coercion, crushed any freedom of intellect.

Although the Darwinian theory does have a considerable number of opponents, science itself is not under attack. We are not about to return to the Dark Ages as some hysterical commentators are claiming.

We have heard the recent complaints of biologists to the apparent organised challenge, in classrooms, to the Darwinian theory of evolution. In sly propaganda or panic maybe, we hear statements that science is under wholesale attack, which of course it isn't. No parent is going to allow their child to die, by refusing medication, because science has provided the means and remedy. It's obviously just a desperate ploy to try and support another tottering hypothesis.

When scientists, in opposition to Mr. Yung's work, and through unproven speculation, attempt to undermine the whole basis and foundation of human life and consciousness, not through any 'self-evident proof' but through irreverent desire, then of course it is only sensible to ask questions. The more penetrating the better. Register what is provable and repeatable and call it science, speculation belongs to science fiction.

Boyle's law, Archimedes' principle, the binomial theorem are not at question here, for they are, as examples – demonstrable. What is becoming heavily questioned and substantively denied is mainly; that 'natural selection' can at anytime lead to a totally new genus, a totally new creature. It just isn't possible.

Neither does this persistent questioning, necessarily emanate from an impugned religiosity, but mainly surfaces, from the injustice of portraying as fact the extremely suspect Darwinian hypothesis.

We have recently witnessed intelligent and qualified men studying a number of same family adults with severe balancing difficulties, (probably genetic brain abnormality.) Unable to remain upright, these adults use their hands and arms to help walk themselves forward. In their desperate attempt to find 'proof' of Darwinian theory, scientists have concluded that these individuals are 'genetic throwbacks to our ancestors' and 'more suited to tree walking.'

We are also informed,

'They display the crude balance of our ancestors.' No forest primate could ever have had 'crude balance,' he would fall out of the tree and kill himself.

While some scientists have distanced themselves from such claims, others have readily stated,

> 'The religionist will not accept the reality
> of evolution – that man originally walked
> on all fours.'

Man, in his life on the planet, has never walked on all fours. There has never been such a creature as a human quadruped, or a bipedal upright ape. The bipedal human has forty six chromosomes to the cell; the quadruped ape has forty eight. The biped is just what the word says it is, and so is the quadruped.

And it's not religion or symbolism that directs us to such conclusion. It's the plain and obvious lack of any evidence to support Mr. Darwin's suppositions. It's the distrust of a speculation dressed up in high sounding names and spoken of as fact, by earthbound men and women with little insight it seems, into the metaphysical, the transcendental, or even the way a disabled person uses anything available to remain mobile. If that means using both arms and legs, that will also be done.

In their rush for 'proof' we can see scientists of the Darwinian persuasion, seduced by this scientific paper referring to 'human quadrupeds.' We can hear the thinking,

> 'This is it, this is the proof we've been waiting for. This will silence the religionist once and for all.'

Children, in their development from crawling to walking, sometimes bumble along on all fours for a time, using arms to steady themselves until of sufficient strength to remain upright. This is stated as being more 'evidence' of the evolutionary process, where human beings supposedly progressed from walking on all fours, to being upright. Further farce of course, with ego demanding the suspension of critical analysis.

The Darwinian fundamentalist does not base his sweeping 'evolutionary' generalities on evidence or even intuition, but on the machinations of reason, and reason can lead us anywhere, to any falsehood our temperament, privilege or prejudice demands.

The religious fundamentalist steadfastly clings to the literal letter of scriptural writings, although many are of obvious symbol and metaphor. The scientific fundamentalist steadfastly clings to an unproven contrivance of mind.

Within any prevailing cultural interpretation of creation, whatever it may be, lies the comforting emotion of conformity. Both the religious fundamentalist and the scientific fundamentalist are one and the same, both have the same need to conformity. The trappings and detail of the verbal or mental constructs are but a communal convenience. Nonconformity is always an irritation, if not a fear, to the conformist.

Hand in hand with the need to conformity goes the need to uniformity. The uniformity of present theory is in itself a powerful attraction. Psychological comfort and security can often lie in the unified belief of the many, to such an extent that even intelligence at times, is no guide to any truth.

Although we may presently be unaware of the universal laws instigating species change and genus inception, the hypothesis of a higher power involved in creation, from a rational point of view, makes more sense than mutation and chance being responsible for the complex myriad life forms we see all around us.

Just a brief glance at a schematic of the human immune system and its complex functioning alone, must impress even the most ardent Darwinist that accident, chance and mutation as instruments in its formation, is not likely to convince everyone.

The enormous variation of biological form doesn't happen for no reason. As a naturalist, it appears Mr. Darwin, and now many of his contemporaries, have sought the answers to creation within the vagaries of rationality and within the limited knowledge of the day.

The circumscribed deductive mind of man can only reveal what is within its boundaries of perception, outside that boundary it guesses at, it makes it up, it maddens itself with one 'improved' fabrication after another. We are informed for example, with studied surety, that 'the building blocks (gases, minerals etc.) made themselves into life.'

In many sections of Western intelligentsia there is an obvious lack of mature understanding of who we are and how we relate to an underlying consciousness that pervades all life in this universe. If we need to forsake, for a few months, heated homes and full bellies, live in hair shirts and eat dry bread and cheese, to focus the mind on these twin factors, then let it be.

Mr. Darwin did insist that his theory of slow step by step linear evolution would require innumerable fossils of transitional form. The heated debate as to what constitutes transitional form, continues unabated. The supposed slow change of fish to tetrapod (fin to foot) for example, through various fossils, is continuously challenged.

If we can't find unequivocal and multiple fossil specimens of the assumed sequential development from ape to man, a supposed development so close to home, then how much more difficult is it going to be, when considering bit-part fossils hundreds of million of years old.

The Archaeopteryx is deemed by the evolutionist to be a transitional form between reptile and bird. It may be odd looking to our eyes and although having teeth similar to other birds of the day, it did have a tail containing vertebrae and is unique in that respect, as is the egg laying platypus, as is the bat, the only flying mammal. The Archaeopteryx was a fully organised independent warm-blooded bird with wings and feathers and probably existed as a species for millions of years.

From soft-bodied sea animals to the early hard shell arthropods, from invertebrate to vertebrate, should both have produced vast numbers of transitional forms over the millions of years of the proposed 'evolution' by Mr. Darwin. None have ever been found.

It is probably beyond most laymen to go trawling through, say the 'membrane instantous in heterotic M-theory' of the evolutionary biologist, but something does feel seriously amiss with this idea of complex material creation happening through mutation, accident or chance. Even mathematicians don't seem able to agree on the probability of that chance.

And like branches springing from a hypothetical

tree, we have ring species, cline species, reproductive isolation, genetic drift, flounder flush, adaptive radiation, sympathetic speciation, and on and on it goes.

If the initial premise is suspect then everything that follows must be suspect as well, however grand the babelous 'new' language may be, and however strong the longing by the contemporary evolutionist, to retain the authority of Darwinian theory.

Slow progressive evolution, through gene mutation and the gene survival and fertile replication, must be questioned and could, if retained, eventually lead to contempt for areas of scientific expertise, and possible unjust hostility toward scientists themselves, as programmed cell death (apoptosis) becomes ever more revealed. For the benefit of us all, any specialist with any doubt in Darwinian theory (and there must be many) has both a moral and ethical obligation to air those doubts.

Cyclopia is again a rare mutation, where the human is born with just one eye in the centre of its forehead. Some have wrongly informed us that this malady is a throwback to a past millennia where upright creatures walked the earth with but one eye. A regeneration, we are told, of a past variation of the species. Yet again, we see the devastation mutation brings in its wake, for the faulty gene responsible for this mutation is a gene that balances the equal development of each side of the body. In its failure, the face collapses, the brain is deformed and most offspring are stillborn.

If we cannot, in any way, appropriate the millions of

haemoglobin molecules within a single cell to arbitrary mutation then how much more difficult is it for us to appropriate to mutation, the conveyance of the light spectrum through the variable focal length eye lens onto the hundred million retinal light cells. Electrical impulses then being passed into the brain, the ensuing impressions or 'picture' inverted and then converted into knowledge of the material world through the consciousness.

We are expected to believe with blind faith that just the eye alone for example, is the result of accident, chance and mutation, paralleled we must remember in each and every species and there are some four to five million separate species. Again a double mutation at exactly the same place and time, for each species.

This eye problem, Mr Darwin did say, gave him a 'cold shudder.' The same cold shudder, one would suppose, as did visit the religious clerics unable to fit the facts of an unfolding cosmology into their flat-earth centre-of-the-universe theory, which was unashamedly preached for hundreds of years by the ruling priesthood, even after it was known to be false.

While most scientists appear to support the present concept of a mechanistic universe, physicist Sir James H. Jeans seems to support the position against a purely mechanistic universe,

> 'We discover that the universe shows evidence
> of a designing or controlling power - - - - - - -
> which for want of a better word we describe as
> Mathematical.'

To retain credibility within his or her own profession a scientist must use acceptable terminology, even if with a capital letter. More encompassing maybe; the word 'Mind,' is obviously too close for comfort to spirituality or Sunday morning worship.

The word 'Mathematical' with its capital letter gives us insight into the 'alternative' thinking by Sir James Jeans while at the same time having to deflect the possible or probable accusation of being a religionist or non-scientific. All professions have their demarcation lines. But it is a truth, that to try and assess the multiplicity of form and its existence, with only a mechanistic appreciation, is like trying to assess distance, blind in one eye.

The reason one scientist and not another, with the same or similar background and experience, gravitates to a conviction of a higher power is obviously not the result of qualification or intelligence alone, and is rarely logic; the mystery lies much deeper than that. But at its heart, appears to be an ever increasing awareness of an originating energy or consciousness, inherent in all life, in all matter.

The obtaining of a professorship or doctorate may indicate a capacity to memorise or reason but it is equally apparent that qualification in any discipline, doesn't automatically endow us with insight into the transcendental. Without temporal lobe activity our vision is limited, our 'knowing' unavoidably isolated to the corporeal.

To return for a moment to the discredited and defunct theory of 'acquired characteristics' which is today, still unthinkingly repeated with revered affection by those who should know better.

It is often that the plausible holds no truth. We are told for instance that our love of fatty foods is the result of those of our ancestors who were successful in obtaining sufficient fats in their diet and then passing on their acquired taste down the generations and into the cultures of today.

The adult human body needs about thirty per cent of its calorific intake to be fats in the form of unheated, unrefined natural nut or vegetable oils, fish oils, or cooked poultry for example, if meat is consumed. Without them our immune system will fail and we die.

The characteristics and potential variation of every species of creature is set at inception. The sentient creature may adjust its diet to utilise the seasonal availability of foodstuffs. The rodent comes to mind or to a lesser extent the adaptable and amiable jackdaw, but passing on the biological need for the oils of the nut, olive, sunflower or even animal flesh, is surely not acquired, but inherent. Qualified commentators really shouldn't be dispensing discredited and redundant theory.

After a severe case of Deep Vein Thrombosis in 2004 and the subsequent careful study of dietary habits, it is apparent that the hydrogenation of oils, fats and proteins to extend product shelf life, and used in cooking oils, margarines and confectionery for over fifty years, has been most dangerous to health.

Inverting another half-baked 'test and proof' belief, namely, that saturated nut oils are dangerous to health, we see that those early tests on hydrogenated oils, levelled any blame for serious ill health at the saturated fat or oil itself and not the trans-fatty acid resulting from the hydrolysing process. A trans-fatty acid never before seen by the human body in all its long history.

It is to be expected that this potentially dangerous product, will be as stealthily withdrawn as it was introduced, with little or no admittance of its dangers.

Raw unadulterated coconut oil is almost wholly saturated fat (medium chain molecule) and is now seen as one of the healthiest foodstuffs on the planet.

A wholesome food, supplied in its purest form, by an excellent firm – Coconut Connections in the U.K.

From lying in a bed in acute admissions at the Carmarthen General Hospital, to twelve months later. The elimination of all hydrogenated fats and oils from daily diet, and substitution with raw coconut oil, fish oil (with brand name – 'Eskimo 3') and walnut oil, along with a gradual build up to a brisk one mile a day swim at the local swimming pool, helped in something like a restoration to health.

The above information is given in good faith and from my own experience. It behoves me to say that the responsibility must lie with the reader to seek medical advice for any ailment, illness or the ingestion of any food supplement, especially if already taking prescribed medicines.

And while on this subject, it should also be stated, the obesity we witness around us, is again nothing to do with acquired characteristics or the ample availability of foodstuffs. Excluding hypothalamus dysfunction, corpulence, it seems, is more to do with emotional and mental upset. A cultural failure which few would wish to reveal, and even fewer, it appears, wish to confront.

Overeating is mostly a compensatory comfort to temporarily suspend our inner pains or loneliness. It is more likely that in a materialistic land of plenty we are reluctant to face our isolation. While the bowl of our biological need overflows, our spirit weeps.

Even though the mind may reel back in awe and ungrasping, we may yet contemplate the enormous reaches of the universe, the immense densities of neutron stars where just a diced sized lump will weigh many millions of tons, or the sheer magnitude of the forces evident in the cosmos.

With these extraordinary wonders before us, it is still possible to understand that if ego is sufficiently self-centred, it could conclude that the universe is but the result of a rolling cosmic inevitability. A belief that the whole cosmos has come into existence without any governance aback of the physical universe. What is much more difficult to understand however, is the unshakable insistence that chance, accident and mutation are responsible for the complex forms of biological life and its reproduction, as both were obviously 'born' together.

Again, even as a theory, the existence of a higher power is inevitably going to seem far more feasible than the contemporary evolutionary theory, of random mutation, chance and accident being the motive force in the precise biological complexity of varying life form.

And are we not told by the biochemist that even at the microscopic level 'unbridgeable' chasms exist, which challenge belief in accident, chance and mutative slow evolution. Again we are looking for that illusive Piltdown man, but this time in the world of the microscopic.

To the rather straightforward question as to why we don't see the innumerable transitional forms his theory demands, Mr. Darwin gives a straightforward answer,

> 'The answer lies mainly in the *(fossil)*
> record being incomparably less perfect
> than is generally supposed.'

One does have to sympathise with this statement of a fossil record less than perfect. For example, there is no fossil record of any coelacanth less than one hundred thousand years old, at least there wasn't at the time a living coelacanth was fished out of the sea in 1938. The coelacanth, to the evolutionist, is 'the fish that walked out of the sea to become the ancestor of us all.'

With no fossil evidence at all of slow step by step evolution, Mr. Darwin maintained,

> 'there can hardly be a doubt.'

of sudden development he maintained,

'ought not to be made without strong evidence'

A little biased and wishful maybe?

Because fossil records appear to reveal an instantaneous eruption of new species, those in the past who sought answers to creation, devised the theory of 'spontaneous generation.' That is, to corroborate the known fossil record, any new species had to be the product of spontaneous and instant creation. A creation emanating forth from eructating mud, bolts of lightening, explosions and the initial convenient gathering, all in perfect atomic order of all the elements needed to produce the complexity of all forms of life.

Spontaneous generation has presently been rejected which means that the scientist has to remain wedded to the present theories. So much so, that whispered comment within the scientific professions is questioning their own 'close minded thinking so long abhorred.'

It is more than likely that in the event of environmental catastrophe or the immanent threat of genus (or even species) extinction, there could be a mechanism within each genus to instant huge swings in variability. A survival mechanism, where variation itself goes into overdrive. An instant (one generation maybe) massive proliferation of variant form, yet still within the relevant variation boundary. Species survival, when under such terminal threat, becoming everything. A simple suggestion that may find fertile ground, there again it may not. The lack of any intermediate forms between genus and genus however, still remains.

Another issue that must be addressed by the ardent evolutionist, is that, of all the millions of species on the planet today of plant, animal, insect, bird and reptile or even the microbe, nowhere do we find a partial species form, and doubt as to where it belongs. Mr. Darwin's idea that the sea otter can be seen as a transitional form because it feeds on land and in the sea, surely can't seriously be considered.

This proposition does in itself however, serve as an example of how feeble is this bubbling pot of jumbled up assumptions that men of learning have so greedily grasped and have so readily accepted, yet are obviously unsound.

Albeit with some limitation, of the huge number of fossils now unearthed, it does appear difficult to obtain any uncontested fossils of transitional forms, or intermediate links between one species and another.

One would have thought, from a logical point of view, that if 'evolution' has taken place in this step by step linear, gradual progression, as expressed by Mr. Darwin, then the shores, deserts, caves and valley floors would be littered with such graduating changes, that have supposedly happened over the last six hundred million years. Logic dictates that there should be enormous numbers of unequivocal links, species to species. In fact, for slow sequential evolution, through mutation, to be correct, there should be little else.

It cannot be presumed that these links just haven't

been found and still lie buried in fossil form. Mr. Darwin also tells us that unless the whole chain of links is found, each end of the chain will be viewed as a separate species. In fact each unconnected link will be viewed, as a separate species.

To conclude this chapter we must consider that if there were no biological constriction of species through the process of variation, through gene type and through chromosome count, then we would have chaos in the natural world, but what we see is order. Ape giving rise to ape, bird to bird, ant to ant, snail to snail.

However, the mechanism that gives us great leaps in form from genus to genus, from one chromosome count to another and from one gene type to another, is not answered by the processes of natural selection. For natural selection is confined to variation and variation is confined to genus.

With variation isolated within the genome, the 'how' of the multiplicity of life form is again, not answered by mutation, accident or chance, which leaves us with the thorny question. With no sample or pattern to copy, how is a complex new genome formed? These are issues that desperately require debate. Yet debate itself must not become an issue it appears, for 'By debating' one professor informs us, 'you give the opposition the platform they seek.' A battle of wills it seems, rather than a battle for the truth.

Having stated that slow sequential evolution with mutation, accident and chance as its motive power, appears to be incorrect, I have no knowledge of the mechanical law(s) operating in the formation of new genus. That in itself doesn't give authenticity to the present evolutionary theory, which does appear to be, in many ways, an ideology masquerading as science.

A single proposal that could be made, is that consciousness plays a part in the development of the multiplicity of life form. A consciousness innate and part of every organism, just as it is innate and part of every cell. It could also be suggested that until some aspect of consciousness is integrated into any formulation for the explanation of genus creation or genome origination, mechanistic explanations alone, will always be erroneous.

Behind the facts of biological variation and the various but circumscribed life forms it can generate, the mystic will ask us if matter can form into anything meaningful without pre-existing consciousness, or, even if matter can itself, generate human intelligence. To both these questions his own answer will have always been no.

So, from his sojourns into the hinterland of the awe inspiring natural world of his earthly abode, he returns, and finds his rest in the comfort of a different order, another beautiful land, but this time of stillness and prayer, gratitude and praise.

CHAPTER EIGHT

FURTHER TO THE DARWINIAN THEORY

'If our theory is true, it is indisputable that before the lowest Cambrian strata was deposited, long periods elapsed, and that during these periods the world swarmed with living creatures.'

Mr. Charles Darwin

It is always possible a single cell was the first life to regenerate on earth. From fossil records, the explosion of complex life seems to have begun with fully formed, completed, altogether compound invertebrates in the Cambrian Period for no prior complex ancestry can be found even in hundreds of feet of earlier rock.

Soft jelly-like multicelled organisms have come to light but no ancestral form of the early prolific hard shell crustaceous animals can be found in pre-Cambrian rock. At one stage Mr. Darwin eagerly snatched at mistaken fossils from very early strata, which later proved to be crystalline formations. His disappointment must have been weighty indeed, his earlier excitement,

'the difficulties are greatly
diminished or even disappear'

so rudely erased.

However, from subsequent finds, it does appear that

Mr. Darwin was correct in assuming the proliferation of life prior to the Cambrian Period, albeit soft-bodied sea creatures. Whatever evolutionists like to propound, there is no fossil ancestry of the hard-shelled arthropod.

The invertebrate and vertebrate types are independently created by whatever means, that is what the fossil record is telling us. In fact, not just telling us but standing on our toes and shouting in our ear, yet most are still unwilling to listen.

A fervent Darwin evolutionist and professor, bending to the evidence of the fossil record eventually had to concede that the main genera of animal, insect, bird and reptile have appeared instantaneously. He then proceeded to tell us that a bird must have somehow hatched from the egg of a reptile. It's here I have to kneel, not in prayer it has to be said, but to sink my teeth into the timber windowsill for a moment or two.

Further, like the child repeated puzzle of which came first the chicken or the egg, we have another conundrum for the chance minded materialist, as to which came first DNA or protein.

A particular protein is formed of a chain of amino acids, and the particular variety and sequence of amino acids in that chain are formed by the synthesising of the DNA molecule.

Organic life needs protein to survive and reproduce, and that protein cannot be formed without the 'instruction' of the enormously complex DNA string or helix. The DNA therefore is instrumental in the reproduction of protein which becomes part of the organic reproductive process of replicated DNA. It's a closed loop circulating in one direction only, for protein itself cannot produce DNA and DNA must have a living organism containing protein to replicate.

So did chance and accident not only create both complex DNA and protein independently, and then somehow bring them together and somehow inject life into the article, or is there some other process responsible for this awesome sequence of creation. In an effort to support preconception, the speculation that mutation, chance and accident are the motive forces, appears very tenuous indeed, unless of course, both DNA and protein came to earth from outer space in some sort of survival shell or radioactive resistant capsule. If so, then the problem remains, but one step removed.

Any dispute it seems, is about, on the one hand, an ordered yet circumscribed process of variation within each and every genus, while on the other, a whiz-bang haphazard development of form and human intelligence through genetic mutation, chance and accident. And that form surviving because of greater suitability to its immediate environment, and then its continuation through fertile replication within the boundaries of an exacting chromosome count and gene formation.

And further, as we run back down the ever widening beam of manifesting human variation do we arrive at a single point emitter anyway – Adam and Eve or just a small group. Could it be as simple as that, for evidence of any early gradation or steps in Homo sapiens 'sequential evolution' along its own line, is again, non-existent. An enigmatic head scratching mystery to those who refuse to consider the probability, that the upright creature 'leapt' onto the planet.

If a lifetime is spent absorbed in energetic search for a leprechaun and one isn't found, then we do have a mystery, a mystery of our own making.

Mentation, human learning, artistic flair, arithmetic understanding and social improvement have often been referred to as human evolution. At inception the Homo sapiens had this innate potential. Learning and cultural development are only possible when built on a potential already existing within the 'boundaries of variation' of the creature, and don't extrapolate into 'evolution.'

Through curiosity and discovery, honest men and women of the sciences when vocal and unswayed by prejudice, peer or sponsor, are becoming increasingly doubtful, that mutation, chance and accident are the driving force behind the wondrous multiplicity of animal, insect and plant life on this planet.

Many scientists faced with such beautiful complexity of form and its reproduction; do conclude that there has to be some sort of higher power responsible for the order and regulation at the molecular level even if through unbreachable physical laws.

Simple deduction carries us forward to a similar conclusion that the same higher power must also be present at the macrocosmic level. As life proceeds from life so intelligence proceeds from intelligence.

It is always difficult to understand how the majestic sweep of life, even if only understood at the intellectual level, does not induce a sense, that somehow, somewhere, governance is involved in its formation, and law in its continuation. A governance the other side of creation.

This whole issue seems to revolve around the single probability that sentiency, in all its manifest forms, has an originating governance as well as mechanical law. If ego cannot admit to this possibility, then the intellect will be used by the errant will as an instrument for fabricating and forging denial.

In an attempt to pacify and silence both the suspicious professional and obdurate layman who will not blindly accept this hypothesis of a mutation driven evolution, it appears an old outgrowth of Mr. Darwin has resurfaced. Apparently a deal is on the table, if troublemakers will just shut up about the paucity of fossil evidence and stop picking at the scabs of the present theory of mutated creation, then a concession can be made. That an Intelligence created a single cell and seeded the planet at the very beginning of time and then left it to evolve exactly as the present theory states, and as that conveniently absent Intelligence knew it would. A fabrication is very much like a lie, only further lies can support it.

This regurgitation appears to have been once again brought into prominence as the 'no life can exist in space' becomes recognised as just another 'scientific' guess-at-it, for we are also told, that space, outer space, includes organic molecules in untold numbers.

Space it seems is a plenum and the universe teeming with microbial life. It is yet to be revealed that the universe is equally teeming with intelligent life, as is presently known in certain circles. The universal disposal of bacilli in space, locked into comets mainly, was proposed in a model by professors Hoyle and Wichramasinghe over forty years ago.

The toughness and resilience of the bacillus has been known for some time. It has recently been reported that bacilli taken from the stomach of a bee have been cultivated under laboratory conditions. The bee itself having been encased in amber, unlikely as it may seem, for some thousands of years.

If this is not some sort of prank or caddish April fool joke then it really is something to parallel the ability of bacilli to survive pressures up to three thousand atmospheres (45000 lbs./sq. ins.) and also survive huge doses of radiation and very high and very low temperatures. Life really is persistent.

Biochemist and Nobel Prize winner Professor Ernst Chain, who isolated and purified penicillin and became one of the founding fathers of the antibiotic, opposed Mr. Darwin's theory from the point of view of his own research. He describes the theory as 'a very feeble attempt' to explain the origin of species. So feeble in fact, he went on to say that 'it can hardly be called a theory.'

Either we have a slow, progressive linear change, with multitudinous intermediate forms, as Mr. Darwin has suggested, their fossils readily available. Or, we have rapid biological and physiological change and the instant inception of new species, when obviously no interconnecting forms (fossils) would exist.

The slow evolutionary path of Mr. Darwin's theory doesn't need an originating consciousness, but logically does need numerous intermediate fossils, or links, plus a sensible explanation for the beginnings of new genus.

The fast or instant biological change or inception, quite obviously won't have interconnecting fossils but now needs, either a universal governance of some sort, or, a different mechanistic means of creation, which neither Mr. Darwin nor anybody else has provided.

And therein, it appears, lies the dilemma.

From the existing available scientific evidence we cannot dismiss the possibility that genera are the result of instantaneous creation. There is no indication, other than hypothesis, that genera are the result of a slow step by step linear evolution.

The Darwinian theory looks very much like a youthful, imaginative intellectual adventure based on an initial assumption of a barren universe, creating out of its own deadness the wonders of space, time and consciousness, with the enormous variety of life form resulting solely from chance mutation.

It should also be stated that we can at times be extremely parochial and see intelligence solely as the ability to problem solving, or the ability and speed to learn and use reason.

The human body itself is the most extraordinary chemical processing factory. The organs alone perform their billions of tasks with such rapidity and accuracy for the lifetime of the creature, we are compelled to ask once again, does inert matter itself, generate the 'intelligence' or 'body consciousness' we can associate with the awesome rapidity and accuracy of ion selection that constantly takes place within the human body. And is this recognition and selection, as the present evolutionary theory asserts, the result of chance mutation rearranging an already healthy cell structure.

We could also make consideration, that within its larger brain, the Neanderthal was more intelligent than the Homo sapiens, even if of greater body mass. It appears the Neanderthal showed little inclination to the forming of complex social structures, but that doesn't mean it was unintelligent or non-analytical.

Nature is usually quite economical in her utilisation. A large brain even with a larger body mass is not created to lie redundant for one million years, as was scientifically supposed of the appendix, until recently.

It could be tentatively speculated, that while not exploiting its deductive intelligence to the same degree as Homo sapiens, the Neanderthal had larger temporal lobes. Could it have had greater knowledge of the universal metaphysic and was that where its greater intelligence lay. It would in itself, not have been the type of intelligence to create monument of its vision.

In our ungodly haste to parade a 'superiority,' we also parade a terrible hubris. A hubris partly instrumental in the destruction of the Neanderthal, as it was with the persecution and destruction of the native North American Indian.

The propagated mental pictures we have of the Neanderthal are of a hairy brute, bent forward as if in the advanced stages of a debilitating spinal disease. This stooping image cultivated, to simulate the gait of apes and thereby deliberately bolster or reinforce, through this image, the doctrine of slow step by step evolution. The Neanderthal, we can be sure, was an upright biped from inception.

The demise and extinction of the Neanderthal was probably the result of multiple effects. Firstly the persecution by Cro-Magnon (contemporary European). Then the creature's innate and hereditary need to live in small clusters or family groups, to become more and more separate.

And finally, because of a culminating propensity to mainly shoreline or coastal habitation the terminal extinction some eleven to twelve thousand years ago by an enormous global tsunami type wave, generated by the entrance into the solar system of a near planet-size (although fragmented) interstellar object. A wave of such unimaginable power; no living thing could survive such onslaught.

The immense list of detail confirming such global catastrophe is convincing indeed, and learnedly related by Messrs. Allan and Delair in their writing 'When The Earth Nearly Died.' This comprehensive and admirable work further questioning scientific 'certainties.'

The press within a species, if it has both persistence and magnitude, could be the primary impulse preceding the instantaneous snap of new form. This sequential evolutionary theory of Mr. Darwin being increasingly denied, as has been, in the past, lifeless intergalactic space, slow climate change, time as a constant, the separating of energy and matter, the finite universe, the theories of the uniformity of nature. And then we have had infant malleability, until recently, part of an 'unquestioned dogmatic teaching,' – that gender was malleable in the young under two years of age. Even with no chromosomal knowledge, laymen knew this to be but further fabrication and crackpot invention.

In the new Hubble inspired model of the universe even stellar evolution is now muted in some scientific circles as 'an elaborate fiction.' What is the world coming to, my lovely old aunt would often ask.

Another recent scientific certainty, convinced that the brain cell could not regenerate. The brain therefore could not grow, yet the brain of the man is larger than that of the child. A strange belief indeed, for if the brain grows in size, then to those of question, it did appear that the brain must have grown additional brain cells.

After quite a long period of creeping consensus and furtive inversion, we are now loudly informed that, 'the brain is the most regenerative organ in the body.'

We really do need a return to the stocks, to discourage the haughty from promoting falsehoods as fact. The prospect of head and face plastered with rotten tomatoes and even more rotten eggs, launched by the unlettered, is bound to lead to the rapid withdrawal of suspect theory touted as fact. The search for fame and prize then based on greater substance.

It is said Galileo brought the troubles he was beset with, upon himself by being tactless. It was the truth that brought Galileo to persecution and imprisonment. Almost three hundred years elapsed after the publication of 'On the Revolutions of Celestial Spheres' by Copernicus, before the ruling authority, the church, officially accepted the truth of celestial mechanics, as initially released in that document.

Although still subject to debate, it is suspected that Copernicus deliberately delayed publication until the year of his death to avoid criticism or even persecution by the church. He knew the truth of celestial mechanics and the falsehoods preached by the then earthly power, which lay at the time within Vatican walls. Bruno would not recant his espousal of Copernicus truth. He was put to death. But not before an iron spike had been driven through his jaw, tongue and palate.

As a final comment concerning the indoctrination of Darwinian theory as fact. It is for the individual to witness and personally forsake the fallacies propagated in each and every ideology, in each and every age. To reach for that personal truth that lies within, has no politic, is not derived from ego, and offends only those who blindly live in their own particular brand of cultural theocracy, whether of nation-state, science or religion.

And, until those of threat, who propagated the theory of a static earth at the centre of the universe, return to apologise to the unempowered but wiser, then no speculation should be accepted as the backbone of any science. Science should not be a question of disproving any and every witty speculation, but should only concern itself with rigorous test and proof. If no proofs exist then to repeat, classify it aright. At best it is but concept, scientific concept maybe, but concept nonetheless. At worse, it is but shallow speculation to gratify and uphold psychological perversity.

And anyway, science of itself can never give opinion into the nature of reality, for that nature is not evident to the five sense intelligence. The material world of the senses is but a world of shadow with its own observable atomic form.

It is but a personal proposal, only for individual consideration, that if 'evolution' means anything, it means the birth of a successive species on the one part, due to the inner and persistent (or even desperate) press from within the preceding species itself, and on the other an unseen, or as yet, an unknown responding universal law.

With no evidence to prove it so, maybe the elephant can become the sea cow, the reptile become the bird and the ape become the man, but surely not through mutation, chance or accident. The longer one studies this issue of mutation, chance and accident being the motive power for biological diversity, the more silly it seems to become.

So to summarise,

1) That 'natural selection' as well as 'lucky selection' can play a part in the slightly different variant forms often found within a genus (family of species).

2) That an in-built genetic variation potential, is the source vital that produces the different species form within a genus.

3) That biological science informs us, mutation can only ever be injurious to an animal, agreeing with Mr. Darwin. Yet evolutionists, opposing their colleagues, insist that mutation is the motive force changing one animal into another, one genus into another.

4) With the tens of millions of certified fossils now in existence, specialists can give us a sensible picture of the life in ages past. And that picture tells us there are no transitional forms and certainly no transitional series, anywhere to be found, in any fossil record of any sort. So many should there be to authenticate the theory, Mr. Darwin uses the word 'numberless.' The fossil record clearly tells us that genera are created separately by whatever means.

5) Mr. Darwin's major mistake was to insist that one genus (kind) can give rise to a totally different genus (one animal turning into something entirely different) through an extension of his natural selection. In six pages 73 to 79 of chapter 4, (Divergence of Character) Mr. Darwin uses the word 'suppose' no less than

twenty times. And in the whole book 'On the Origin of Species' it has been stated that Mr Darwin uses the subjunctive (I believe, assuming, supposing, etc) some eight hundred times.

6) It may not be known to science what power or law creates the self-evident instant snap of an entirely new genus and its entirely new genome, but this power or law is obviously not aimless.

These six points should be carefully considered as they are not the fanciful speculations of those who would like the earth, its life forms and the cosmos in general, to be ordered to their own wish and desire.

We take ourselves with us wherever we go, and unto ourselves we have no choice but to remain true. Whether our intelligence be sufficiently penetrating, our experience sufficiently broad, or our schooling sufficiently fulsome, is not so important.

For the criticism of Mr. Darwin's work, I do make the most sincere apology to him, but has been undertaken because the theory, even to a layman, appears to be wrong. Nevertheless, as necessary as that criticism has been needed to this commentary, I do hope that one day I may shake Mr. Darwin's hand in some small recompense, for his difficulty and pain in contrasting the apparent cruelty of predation, with a Creative Consciousness and its innate love of all its creatures, has mirrored my own inner uncertainties, torments and crises.

CHAPTER NINE

JUST A SMALL CHANGE IN THE GENOME

'The human is a very strange ape'
Mr. Desmond Morris
Zoological Curator

It is a very strange ape indeed, because it isn't an ape at all. Man and ape cannot reproduce, not only because of the difference in chromosome count but also because of the lack of *close genetic banding.*

Different chromosome counts in animals is not a complete block to fertile replication, but it *is*, if there is no close genetic banding, one animal to the other.

The horse kind, as an example, with 62, 64, and 66 chromosomes per cell, can, with interbreeding across the counts, produce fertile offspring but only because of the close genetic banding.

This close genetic banding is a critical factor, for with different or even the same chromosome count and no close genetic banding, no fertile offspring will emerge.

We can have mouse, pig, fox and cat, all with 38 chromosomes (each isolated to their own variation box) yet, because of the obvious lack of close genetic banding there will be no fertile offspring, were any of these to be paired.

The difference in chromosome count, of say one mouse to another, is but the shuffling of genetic information within the mouse variation box; within the mouse genome. Fertile mouse offspring may emerge from the mating of two mice with different chromosome counts but only because both sets of chromosomes are of close genetic banding. That is, within the mouse genome.

The 38 chromosomes of the fox will again have its own box of variation within its own genome – a different genetic banding to the mouse, hence interbreeding of fox and mouse, each with 38 chromosomes, cannot produce fertile offspring.

Also, the wide difference in chromosome counts within the one genome, say the mouse again at between 22 and 40 is but an indication of the wide variation span within the mouse genome, increasing its ability to survive as a species. The same goes for the fox.

So, we can say that the difference in chromosome count *is* a complete barrier to fertile replication, on condition we add the proviso of 'no close genetic banding.' Or, in other words, no one genus can spring from any other.

While reptiles and mammals can have the same number of chromosomes, they can also have entirely different gene formation – tetraploid, diploid and triploid. The cross breeding of such is generally assumed to be utterly impossible.

Of similar genetic make-up to the great apes, the Homo sapiens, we are informed, has a relatively small difference in DNA, yet, is of a vastly different capability and consciousness. These capabilities the human has had for the entirety of its span on the planet. Homo sapiens hasn't evolved in that time to be able to build the Hubble telescope or anti-gravity machines. It has learned according to its potential and that potential was already there at inception.

The Homo sapiens has more recently exploited its broad deductive and analytical capability, its spiritual potential expressed as the Supplant is yet to come. The potential exists before its manifestation.

From swinging naked in the trees to the binomial computer, escaping the gravitational pull of the earth, the Empire State Building and the genius of Tolstoy, Bach, Einstein and Leonardo da Vinci.

All such wonders pre-empted by just a small change in genetic make-up. Such a small change making possible such a large difference in species. An almost unquantifiable difference.

This reputed small difference in DNA between ourselves and the great apes, allows us to create all manner of transport, to develop language and verse, to manufacture precision instruments for use in complex surgery, to have insight into the geometries and mathematics, which enable us to peer into the endless outer reaches of the universe and into past time, as well as the skeletal structures within the body.

Nonetheless we remain territorial, retributive, egotistical, combative and at times brutal. It is surely creditable that even with such impediments we cultivate a civilisation as best we know. We build great cities yet produce the chemical, biological and atomic means for their destruction.

If a small but permanent and hereditary difference in the genome can give us the startling contrast between ourselves and the tree inhabiting primate, then what is the genetic difference needed to eliminate the wretched traits which lead us to war, to savagery, to cunning, guile and cruelty, to control, elitism and privilege, to dominion and despotism. No sane thinker can surely be convinced that this condition can continue, let alone, must continue. And until that nature is metamorphosed, in the biological change that is to come, history will always repeat itself

Tome after tome has been written on how mankind must alter its ways or perish. Man is Man is Man. How can this simple observation ever be overlooked. Is it the fear of who we are or the shame? Both it seems are the 'evolutionary' pressures; part of the press. Man can temper behaviour to suit whatever the prevailing cultural conditions demand, or what they may become, but the power to subjectively alter itself is not within its ambit. The superficial it may change, the nature to unknown prescription – no.

There can be little doubt that genetic manipulation and experimentation in behavioural patterns are being carried out in secret deep underground military establishments around the world, human cloning included.

Yet, by no amount of persistent need or imagination, can any species create, of its own will and volition, an existence of which it cannot of itself comprehend.

From the very heart of man emanates the desire to end the manner of dominion of one man to another. The nature of man is innate and his concrete cognitive selfhood finds hurt and retaliation its lot, even if controlled or veiled in superior wit. Strangely, more socially acceptable, for the will to wound is no less diminished.

The Rabbi Jesus, the Buddha, and the elevated in general have brought doubt and questioning into the retributive nature of Homo sapiens by advocating the obverse – forgiveness. For, if retribution is seen as a veritable vice, then the creature Homo sapiens has not been born aright and we must ask, why in the numerous kingdoms of life on this planet, is man the only creature born amiss. Unless it is a truth, that the inner consciousness has been a latent unseen force, aback of man since inception. A potential, exposed and revealed by the above emissaries, and in their revelations a companion understanding and acceptance by many in every generation thereafter.

To be free of wounding immaturity and the lowly selfhood is the desire that has become paramount, for in that calling lie the seeds of the coming freedom. A freedom beyond measure, not the fanciful dream of the adolescent, but the very nature of the indwelling presence itself. None will ever again suffer the isolation that comes with human ego. Loneliness will never again numb the soul.

Was it the painfully honest Sonny Liston, the one time American boxing champion who said the young of the species were a delight to him, and it was such a pity that as adults they become a pain in the neck.

Wordsworth more eloquently put it so,

> 'The youth who daily further
> from the east must travel.'

These observations of this 'loss of life' of the adult of the species, are in both cases most graphically if differently illustrated.

Ego matures and squeezes out of existence the childhood 'vision splendid.' This loss seems to bring few adults to tears as they strive and struggle for survival or opulence, until age and waning strength often rekindle the elemental insights of long forgotten innocence.

The transformation or transmutation of the dominant ego, releases that which is indwelling to incarnate through the flesh of the coming biological form. Of the holy indwelling consciousness no human ego exists, as it doesn't in that same consciousness to come – The Supplant.

Are you there caterpillar one, over.
What is it caterpillar two, over.
I've just had the weirdest feeling
caterpillar one, that some day we are
going to be able to fly, over.
That's crazy caterpillar two, we're
much too heavy and anyway we don't
have wings, over.
I'm sure your right caterpillar one, it
was such a strange feeling. I really
felt I was somehow different, over.
Give it a rest caterpillar two, over and out.

Men and women tinkering with human DNA at underground facilities worldwide in attempts to create better soldiers and the like, could not even by accident have produced the precise genetic alteration required to initiate the transmutation of ego. Ego that deliberately blots out the holy light and casts its interminable shadow across the face of the species.

Any elevated change in man cannot come from the hand of man himself, for at best he will only repeat what he is. A change in cultural conditions doesn't change human nature, he may adjust his behaviour but the lower selfhood remains. He sleeps with it, he awakes with it.

Left to philosopher we would no doubt have a garrulous self-important, left to the scientist we would have whatever a culture demands, be it the incubator or the atom bomb, while others would present us with a servile compliant.

As long as we allow ourselves to be aware of the contrast within and sincerely wish the dissolution of self-centred egotism, then we can confidently await its eventual passing.

The infant appears to more often experience the spirit of the Supplant to come, before capitulating to the developing ego. In its 'hybrid' organism the Supplant will remain free of this 'maturation.' Paradise? Of course, if we consider paradise as a state of being and not some airy-fairy land in the skies or ether. For truly the infant knows paradise; ego for all its persistent effort does not, and cannot.

My little babe.
Where do you go when
you fall asleep.
Is it heavenly company
that you keep,
In your sublime repose.

Even though we may voice our eternal need to 'live as soul' how many of us have the courage or will, to embrace the humbling possibility that the successor to man already exists, and as a species awaits the rapidly approaching day of its calling. This successor, an angelic soul, silently residing in each and everyone of us, to be fully revealed and expressed on earth in one glorious moment of geological time, ourselves writ large – the coming Supplant.

CHAPTER TEN

BORN ANEW

How can biology affect the spiritual state of the creature we may ask. Well, the whole issue here is that man is endowed with a spiritual nature, a spiritual consciousness of love, tenderness, wonder, wisdom and beauty, and this sensitivity is known to express, in varying degrees through the temporal lobe within the brain. That's as far as science, it seems, presently takes us. Biology does not of course create spirituality; it only allows its manifestation. Music, verse and mathematics existed before the man.

Those who have limited temporal lobe activity have little or no cognition of the inner consciousness. The parietal lobe, again within the brain, we are informed, is of the rational, analytical and cognitive selfhood. With no temporal lobe activity, human ego is not subject to a governing authority to control its excesses. It is then only restricted to any extent, by a self-construct of behavioural conformity so that it may be allowed to function within the prevailing social conditions.

Without this social restriction through law and its enforcement, ego would have no need to use reason to try and mimic the temporal lobe's altruistic balance and would then licence itself to run amok, to run riot, to abuse any who oppose its will or whim. A calamity often multiplied through the unscrupulous use of obedients in the form of an army, especially if they themselves are similarly disabled.

This, it appears, is why the 'certainty' of the atheist (and at times the religious fundamentalist) has throughout history been so dangerous to those of fuller brain function and the fuller perception of universal truths.

So overwhelming becomes the obsessive conviction that nothing exists outside the atomic, the deductive, and the circumscribed five sense consciousness, that the ardent atheist will always attempt to nullify the transcendental, if not by violence then by the insidious use of reason, contempt, ridicule and denunciation.

An unremitting longing, to silence those who openly oppose and reject a narrow-minded materialism and the notion of a single reality, with its concocted teaching of the individual bereft of the spiritual, man as the only self-conscious creature in the universe, and a cosmic devoid of any spiritual dimension.

If a guess was to be made at the genetic change undertaken to launch the forthcoming 'leap' of humankind, it could be conjectured that the genetic change is somehow connected or linked, in part at least, to either an extension or expansion of the temporal lobe(s), or some sort of serious re-energising. But that would only be a guess.

At the opposite end of the spectrum, an inactive temporal lobe inevitably leads to a distorted view of reality, a corporeal mechanistic view.

The Indian seer Sri Aurobindo, with his insight into the forthcoming elevation of mankind, to that of 'superconsciousness' in bodily form, sought answers to the detail of that development, through reason, with some tortuous and speculative hypothesising.

Unable to see, through reason, (he states, 'our only sure guide') quite how this embodiment could take place, Sri Aurobindo in seeming resignation, concluded that planet Earth is unfitted to accommodate such divinity, and its manifest form. That the planet is only able to support an 'inferior order.'

The exact opposite must also demand some consideration, namely, that the planet is much too beautiful to endlessly house the ugliness of egocentricity and the ugly necessity of rigid institution.

From what I have come to understand, succinctly related through the poem, no agreement can be found with this intellectualised conclusion of Sri Aurobindo, that the planet is unfitted for the coming Supplant. This wonderful planet is to be home to the most wondrous and sensitive of creatures, reaching out in love and joy to every creature.

The detail of the genetic manipulation, the Supplant's genetic make-up, is really beyond us and carried out by those of greater capability than ourselves and something that will be commented upon in the final two chapters.

The transformation rather than the dissolution of the Homo sapiens has been undertaken by those of unbounded compassion and wisdom, even if apparently detached.

To suggest disaster to the human race because a more refined and elevated form is to inhabit the planet, is short sighted and little more. As this planet is not the centre of the universe so the creature Homo sapiens is not the summit of creation.

Although the works of Mr. Dean Radin offer us some insight; according to the general understanding of science as presently accepted, there is no known repeatable and instrumentally verifiable indwelling presence or consciousness, although as mentioned earlier, the non-instrumental science of clinical psychology furnishes a different picture. A picture, similar to many an intuitive and spontaneous private experience or insight, and not for circus or laboratory anyway.

In our appreciation of the elevated being, soon to inhabit this planet, it is important to further extend an understanding of this inner consciousness and something of its forthcoming incarnating form, using the verses from the poem related in chapter two, as guidance.

Plough an unwavering furrow
In the ageless field of time
To view the glorious future
Soon to enshrine mankind.

This, the first verse is self explanatory, except that attention should be drawn to the word enshrine, which with delightful pulchritude is described in dictionary with the words – sacred affection. Again we are witness to the universal love of the Creative Consciousness, this time directed towards the creation to come.

None are held in a punishment block awaiting the finger of damnation, as those of primitive need feel compelled to insist. All are welcome, yet many it seems will not wish to be included, but will seek to continue their experiences in the solitude of human ego some place else. (many are called, but few choose.)

To those weary of isolation and witness to the great love of the Father, such needs will have burned themselves out. Their lament is for release and not further incarceration in the narrowness of a five sense consciousness. Our own need will see us where we most long to be. We do create our own future, as we have created our own past.

Where no mother or child sleep hungry
Lest the whole world stand alert
And seeds of rhythm and tranquillity
Are sown in unpoisoned earth.

When men live in unrelenting egocentricity and do not 'see' the Creative Consciousness, in say the preening housefly, or, held in the palm of the hand, the beautiful crystalline structure of the snowflake, or marvel at the breath of the Infinite in the breeze fluttering down a hedgerow, and are not witness to the likeness within themselves, then it is always possible mothers and children will go hungry.

Who is it that carries the greatest burden, he who steals the food from the mouths of distant babes, or he who blames the Infinite for lack of intervention.

When men are witness to the Eternal, both within themselves and without, then none will go hungry and no mother will ever weep in need for her children.

This second verse, graphically describes the coming Supplant, living in a non-coercive social order of unparalleled philanthropy, goodwill and integrity. Where infanthood is one of total security, love and care, and where mind is linked to mind in a pool of awareness of each and every individual need. With written law unnecessary and social benevolence lived fully, minute by minute in the heart of all.

Presently, and in stark contrast, we have Professor Mr. Peter Singer informing us that the new born is not a person because we can't communicate with it, many would vigorously disagree. In an isolating rationalism

Mr. Singer informs us that we can't reason with a newborn, we can't have a discussion about the merits or demerits of utilitarian philosophy, so therefore we can't communicate, so therefore the newborn is not a person.

The newborn as soon as it can focus, in its helplessness immediately searches for the certainty of security in the eyes of its guardian, it is immediately aware of contact with that guardian, and to any guardian that is communication. We cannot fail to have a bonding reaction with such questing eyes.

The least we can say of the newborn is that it is an individual human being, and that makes it, in any language, a person.

Professor Singer then leads us from 'the newborn is not a person' to,

'No newborn has a right to life.'

which allows us to clearly see where reason and ungoverned rationalising leads us. Logic can lead us to the grotesque just as easily as it can lead us to the profound; it is that malleable. To allow logic to govern our lives is heathen.

The acorn is not destroyed because it is not yet the oak, the egg because it is not yet the eagle, the lamb because it is not yet the ewe or the roe because it is not yet the sturgeon.

All newborn human life capable of selfconscious existence, even if physically impaired, demands an obligation from us all. To insist the newborn has no right to life is not so much arrogant in its absurdity, as to be heartless in its conception and suggestive to each and every megalomaniac.

Further, clinically efficient and surreptitious abortion doesn't make it any the less infanticide, when the whole argument hinges on the premise that while in the womb, the foetus is non-human or un-human. A wholesale tragedy of silent and unseen violence.

Could it be, the infant of the womb is aware of its mother's love and cherishing. If that is so, then it could also be aware of the rejection of abortion. Because we don't know the nature of our multi-faceted consciousness, can we be certain that the foetus is unaware of its impending doom.

A child returns

It seems but yesterday oh mother,
a fever wracked and claimed me.
Grief was thine in my sudden passing,
and so heavy was thy heart,
so unremitting was thy sorrow.
In the endless panorama of time
the Almighty has once again
bound us as one.
Yet now you seek to slay me.
What has happened,
what could have happened
that you would hate me so.
I beg thee dear mother
do not rip me from thy body.
In your arms cradle me again.

As distressing as it is, we cannot wilfully deny and destroy the foetus and expect peace of mind in our lives or the happiness of the unborn.

Where no living thing be hunted
No cunning, stealth or lures
Wild birds alight on tender hand
And protecting arm secures.

In this, verse three, the relationship of the Supplant to the animals is quite clear and again further revealing of its inviolate and unrefractive nature.

Although not able to share the vast consciousness of the Supplant, the forest animal will no doubt rejoice in the company of this virtuous and noble being.

In ignoble contrast we have an unidentified executive or committee responsible for increasing the level of CJD in the human population, with the filthy practice of feeding ground down scrapie infected carcases to ruminants and herbivores. Scrapie in sheep being a close microbial cousin of CJD. It takes a very special indifference indeed to even dream-up such a vile practice, let alone implement it.

It really is difficult to understand such indifference when all creatures are inherently fascinating to the human spirit, and like children can forever keep us enthralled. Feeding pulped apple or grape to wasps, off a summer garden table and surrounded by these enchanting creatures, the terror that a single wasp engenders in adults is again extremely difficult to understand.

As an historic expression of a facet of the Supplant consciousness, it appears St. Francis of Assisi had a remarkable and intimate relationship with mute creatures. There is a lovely account of this saintly man and most edifying it is, in just the telling.

An exceptionally large and hostile wolf, through hunger, had become a threat and understandably all in the locality were frightened and wished to have it destroyed by some means.

Having walked to the edge of the village with the fearful villagers St. Francis proceeded on foot, alone, towards an area where the wolf was thought to be. As St. Francis approached the beast, it charged at him with teeth bared. St, Francis, unperturbed, stood his ground and on making the sign of the cross in its face, the wolf halted its charge and stood still. He called the animal to him whereupon it lay at his feet.

He spoke kindly to the subdued wolf and eventually took it to the village square where all could see it closely. He made the people promise to feed the animal daily, and he asked the wolf to promise that never again would it attack either people or other animals. The people watched in disbelief as the huge wolf placed its paw in the hand of St. Francis.

Each day the wolf would enter the village for its daily sustenance without fear of the people and the people having no fear of it. The close friendship of the villagers and the wolf remained until the aged animal eventually died. Even to inveterate animal lovers, it goes without saying really, a whining domestic dog may be one thing, a half-crazed hungry wolf another.

From this account alone it again becomes all too obvious how far we in the Western world of logic and iron, have divorced ourselves from the above events. They become quite unbelievable.

And from the elevated sutras of Patanjali we read,

> 'Near him in whom non-violence has fully taken root, all beings renounce enmity.'

There is also another similar story of a young girl who, to avoid marauding armies, escaped into the forests of Germany during World War Two. Wolves befriended her and although she had nothing to offer them in return, they brought her rabbits and other small mammals on which she survived, eventually returning, alive, to more civilised conditions.

She was quite elderly when relating her moving story on television. This does mean of course that in those days of menace and threat, at least one of us was safer with the wild animal than with her own.

For a very tender vocalising of the fear most wild animals have for man, do listen to the rendition 'Man walks among us' by the late Marty Robbins. Another instance of exquisite expression inherent in the arts.

It has also been speculated or maybe wish-desired that, in the age to come, all predation in the animal kingdom will also cease, but of that nothing is known to me.

Where no country need militia
No borders to divide
War, a distant memory
No despots to misguide.

This verse is again unambiguous and revealing of the unlimited and unconditional philanthropy which in one bound changes the whole face of the planet – literally. With no personal or private ambition, the amassing of armies, the intrigue of secret services and all the paraphernalia of war, become a thing of the past.

From the historic despots of royalty and ancient priesthoods to contemporary parliamentary rule, openness in politics is a suicidal virtue.

> 'He, without moral or ethical principle
> will use deceit and cunning to obtain far
> greater wealth and success, than any of
> integrity and honesty.'
>
> Machiavelli (1469 - 1527)

Although claimed by scholars to be a political theorist, Niccolo Machiavelli based his comments and advise not on invention but on his observations of the play of those around him in power, of both the civil politic and the religious politic. Which means, (if Machiavelli is correct,) that integrity and the obtaining and retaining of earthly power, whatever its shade, never exist together, however mighty the empire, however opulent the architecture or however eloquent the statesman.

The duplicitous use of reason and logic appear to be the pillars upon which all earthly power stands, which prompted the Christ to say, "I am not of this world."

Lethal violence (the taking of life) is morally acceptable if state authorised, argues the Bishop of London, Richard Charters (2004). Within the Christ consciousness no such compromising acceptability exists, and the holy consciousness cannot of itself surrender to the dissolute endeavours of human passion, even if that endeavour is viewed as a lethal necessity. Such things are of the species Homo sapiens, and the Bishop in his office, should have exposed and emphasised this contrast, even if subordinate to state.

And let not the theologian forget, that some of the most wretched atrocities in the history of humankind have been state sanctioned, state sponsored and founded in both dictatorship and democracy.

A theologian may understand the social human need for a self-defence but should never neglect to immediately qualify and contrast the often barbarous results, with the tenderness of the holy indwelling presence. In that blunt contrast the teachings of the Christ are propagated.

'No despots to misguide' brings to mind the history of the ruthless Greek, Alexander of Macedonia. As the name Hitler is synonymous with war so is the name Alexander. War, which always brings with it, hatreds, massacres, and untold grief and misery. It is further stain to blight the species.

Alexander, an aristocratic young man of endeavour, yet the rosy stories of a glorious hero are but the ancient propaganda of the victor. A victor shorn of the dark side of his nature and his drifting into madness – a megalomania that visits all mortals, in proportion to their earthly power.

An honest historian otherwise noted 'All who write of Alexander prefer the marvellous to the true.' The unctuous words of the early scribes repeated in text-books and classrooms throughout Europe.

Although having defeated the Persians years earlier, Alexander was still full of longing to reach the ends of the earth, but his battle hardened, war weary soldiers, after eight years of privation, marching and fighting, expressed their wish to return home from the far lands of India. As this all-conquering army turned, they were on their way home, or so they thought.

It was also written at the time that hundreds died in the following sixty day trek through the hostile and almost waterless Makran desert as the army marched inland from the coast. A Greek historian of the time also tells us otherwise. Of an army of one hundred and twenty thousand men, only thirty thousand survived. Ninety thousand men perished in that desert.

There has to be something desperately distorted about human perception when a general looses three quarters of his army, with no enemy in sight, and is described as 'great.' To a man who has only ever commanded a small kit of poultry, the word idiotic springs to mind. Unless it was, as has been suggested, a deliberate act of vengeance by Alexander towards his trusting men for dashing his personal ambitions.

As one would expect, the Persians were blamed for the death of Alexander but with the debacle of the Makran march and the reneging on his promise to return home (he assembled a fleet of one thousand ships to sail east, just days before he died) it is more probable that a disillusioned high ranking noble killed him, for Alexander didn't see Greece again either – he died in convulsions – poisoned.

Deep-etched no doubt, in the post war memory are the pictures of another without conscience, surveying the conquered lands of an empty French capital and standing victorious before the Eiffel Tower in the summer of 1940.

Sickening as this unabashed lust to conquer and to dominion may be, who will ever forget when told of the fact, that in just one battle of the American Civil War a mother lost five of her sons. How can we speak of honour or courage, wisdom or foolishness, right or wrong, must we only speak of the sorrow.

Hate and retribution are obviously of the lower human emotion, purely a human need or reaction, however well wrapped in theology, liturgy or global organisation.

There can never be a call from the holy consciousness to any man to wound, or to maim, or to seek retribution in its name, no more than a mothering gazelle would encourage its offspring to kill a sibling for being first to a tasty leaf.

A call to arms 'in God's name' is a contradiction in terms, primitive in the extreme and only coined to try and give legitimacy to the bestiality to come. Goodness cannot be culturally or internationally spread through murder and mayhem, or as expressed in rhyme,

Stand erect oh man, but hang thy head in shame.
The pools of blood, the agony, the pain.
With every wound and every dying sigh,
Thou hast made for each a child to cry.

We also have to be careful, not to slip into the view that 'war has its uses' as if of something other than the cruel and brutal.

> 'there is not the least inconsistency between
> loving men and fighting them.'
>
> G. K. Chesterton.

It should be noted how Mr. Chesterton, to soften his message, uses the word fighting when he really means battlefield killing, as if war were but the extension of a playground joust.

While the dual nature of the Homo sapiens may consistently display both love and hate no such duality exists within the indwelling Christ consciousness, to which the statement above would be an absurdity.

Love, in the context given to us by the Christ, does not drive us to slay our fellowman, any more than it does a mother to slay her firstborn. Compromise and duality are no part of the Christ consciousness.

We also have Mr. Christmas Humphreys, making the following statement in his book – Walk On, page 54,

> 'The individual can only find himself, and integrate his jumble of selves, by constantly sacrificing himself to something he knows and admits to be larger than himself. Many of us learnt this lesson during the war….. *(ww2)*'

Without going into any long-winded critique of the sentiments of Mr. Humphreys, and if I have understood aright, this particular statement does appear to be dangerous ground to either advocate or even consider, for a number of reasons.

Firstly, the training of individuals for war draws the often fragile yet heartfelt attraction to the Christ consciousness, away, in an opposing direction, toward the hardening of heart and the subjugation of mind. Those who seek dominion have known of this propensity in men to reach towards That which is greater than themselves, and usurp and exploit that need to further their own nefarious ambitions.

As has been stated many times, the instigation of war by ruling powers, whether of state, priesthood or aristocracy, is the abuse and usury of a people. No war can exist without the initial formation of a hierarchical social structure. It is no easy task for the idealist to assimilate, that while man has duality within his nature, he will always have a more or less centralised hierarchical structure within his communities, which means he will always have war.

Men will always have war, for the human politic is incomplete without it. Nonetheless let us wish the end of war and conflict, not possible with the Homo sapiens yet certain with the succeeding life to come on earth.

Secondly, the mass gatherings at places like Nuremberg may have been a different order of emotional experience for the populace, but hardly a lasting enlightenment even if we don't consider the rabid motives of the organisers.

And thirdly, it must always be remembered that three times as many American soldiers, home from Vietnam, committed suicide after the war than were killed during it. Hardly a favourable confirmation of Mr. Humphreys' war induced glimpse of enlightenment and certainly not the conviction of many reflective soldiers, inhabiting the rat-infested trenches of the First World War.

Yet, it can often be the case that periods of intense spiritual illumination can come to any, in any situation, even amidst the atmosphere of warring and hostilities. Such experiences would inevitably elevate the ripening individual, whether warring or not.

Many Buddhist commentators speak to us of merit, self-earned merit that carries favour for us. Yet, we must not forget that which also carries us forward, namely the unavoidable and at times intense mental, emotional and physical suffering that is the inevitable result of successive and multiple incarnation.

And when, taking refuge from the bustle of daily life, we solemnly and silently consider the travail and prolonged pain of heart and mind that each generation of the human species has been subjected to for the long period of its history, are we not driven to ask. Does this anguish emanate outwards through the ether into a meaningless blackness of space or inwards to an equally non-existent deity. Or, is each loss, each sadness, each longing, each tear and call, weighed and measured by an unfathomable and incomprehensible Consciousness.

Where charity love and compassion
Are link to ancestral lore
No intent remain a secret
Retribution is no more.

The first two lines of this verse appear to refer to the courageous and persecuted disciples, who sought to promote the essential wisdom and beauty of the perennial truths of the Christ consciousness. In the second two lines we see a dramatic contrast to the instinctive human need to retribution and also the negation of every cherished institution of wig and gown. As part of the inborn character of the coming Supplant, again we see repeated, the unity of mind and the obvious impossibility of deceit.

It is said, the success of the entrepreneur depends upon what he can conceal. He would have no ability or opportunity to conceal his surreptitious need; it could not even be contemplated. The persistence in his need for such conditions, to practise and fulfil his self-oriented ambitions, would ensure he would find somewhere else in the universe more amenable to his desire for privacy of will.

Where the Ancient of the cosmos
To each a gift will bring
All will know their destiny
Death will have lost its sting.

That the Supplant is of protoplasmic biology is quite apparent from this verse, as it does pass away, or die, but now it knows, through its vast consciousness, the processes of incarnation.

As the past, present and future, along with consciousness, are ultimately one, so the Supplant is aware of a oneness about all its incarnations, thereby the death, the parting, the loss, the great divide is also a thing of the past – our present.

Maybe 'a gift' refers to the permanent and continuous awareness of a two-way love with The Heavenly Father, the Cosmic Consciousness. I'm not really sure about this one as it could possibly be the enormous untrammelled aspect of the inner consciousness itself. Transient shadows of it we see as the paranormal, that is, extrasensory perception, telepathy, clairvoyance, psychometry, precognition, telekinesis, psychic healing, astral projection and so on.

We are here, not just speaking of an expansion of consciousness or just an altered nature. We are speaking of the expression of an already existing consciousness in all its divinity, of which the expansion of consciousness is but a part.

Neither is this only about an improved cognitive or deductive intelligence beyond the wildest and most fertile dreams of men. An enormous intelligence, unencumbered by the gamut of the selfish constitution or private ambitions of human life.

It is not about a better man or a man of greater compassion or philanthropy. The Supplant is an entirely different creature with a life agenda far removed from dominion, acquisition and the general vanities of the Homo sapiens.

Again, Indian author Sri Aurobindo while recognising that 'evolution' has a dual thrust, expresses an uncertainty, as to whether man is really capable, even through so-called self perfection, of developing into a 'higher evolutionary being.' Through 'supposition' Sri Aurobindo concluded that the 'being to come' would not be of the human constitution. The Supplant is as distant from ourselves as we are from the tyrannosaurus.

From the heavens issue forth
Ne'er again the Father to eschew
Man, no longer selfish renegade
But a creature born anew.

The Supplant itself is to arrive on the planet from the heavens. This obviously has no connection with the Christian 'heaven' for it is written in the plural. The Christian heaven being a conscious condition of both mind and being, as opposed to a terrestrial or cosmological position in the Solar System.

The 'heavens' in this case, are the skies above the oceans and the land mass. The Supplant is to be delivered from the space we see above us, as a creature 'born anew,' of new flesh. Not of man, not of the planet, but from somewhere beyond.

'For as the lightening cometh out of
the east and shineth even unto the
west: so shall also the coming of the
Son of man (Son of the Holy Spirit) be.'

Matt; chap.24: 1–28.

The cry and press from within the Homo sapiens has been heard in the cosmos. Those that have answered our inner need, our inner press have created the succession. This succession has not been directly created by an anthropomorphic 'out there' God with the swing of a metaphorical index finger, or in this case the spontaneous eruption of new form from within the primary consciousness.

But as the soil converts potential into bloom, so this cosmic intelligence of vastly superior beings is used to convert the potential within the Homo sapiens into the full blossoming of its vast inner consciousness. An inner consciousness fully revealed through new biological form. If a relatively small genetic change can take us from the tree inhabiting primate to the atomic clock then maybe a relatively small genetic change can take us from Animalman to Supplant.

The word 'renegade' from reading and rereading, no doubt, too many cowboy stories as a youngster, always conjured up the picture of a mean unkempt predator of a man, on horseback, outlawed, on the run and hiding in the rocky terrain of the Badlands.

The dictionary describes the word 'renegade' as meaning deserter or apostate and apostate is defined as 'the abandonment of one's religious faith.' So the word renegade more accurately describes someone who has turned his or her back on the eternal and omnipotent Consciousness and regrettably embraced the temporal world of Mammon.

There could not be a more apposite word to describe the contemporary atheism referred to earlier in these pages, be it either active or of ignorance. And renegade is not a word I would have selected myself, for as explained above this is not what I understood its meaning to be. This confession would make any language teacher cringe in horror, nonetheless that is the truth. Again the learning mind isn't a cloned computer programmed by some central comptometer; it is subject to multiple influences both from within and without. Well, that's my excuse anyway.

CHAPTER ELEVEN

ARE THEY HERE?

'They have been tracked on radar screens - - - - - and the observed speeds have been as great as 9000 miles an hour. I am convinced - - - - - - that these objects are not manufactured by any nation on earth. I can therefore see no alternative to accepting that they come from an extraterrestrial source.'

Air Chief Marshal Lord Hugh Dowding
Printed in The Sunday Despatch July 11. 1954

Some weeks later after further questioning on the subject, Lord Dowding added,

> 'Of course UFO's are real - - - - - - and they are interplanetary - - - - . The cumulative evidence for their existence is quite overwhelming and I accept the fact of their existence.'

Lord Dowding was a realist. He would have had to be, as commanding officer of Fighter Command during the Battle of Britain, fourteen years earlier. At the end of the battle for the British Isles, Lord Dowding stood haggard, exhausted and sacked. Others willingly took credit for the victory.

Thankfully some men are naturally open and not given to waffle or connivance. Lord Dowding, to whom we all owe our freedom, was subsequently maligned for the unambiguous statements he made on this subject, or that is how it appears. And whereas Galileo, under sentence of death, withdrew the truth he had earlier revealed, Lord Dowding, not being under the same overt threat, did not. Man is Man is Man, only the cultural decoration changes it seems.

> 'for nearly fifty years the secrecy apparatus in the United States government has kept from the public, UFO and alien information. We have contact with alien cultures.' (note the plural – *cultures*)
>
> Astronaut Dr. Brian O'leary 1994

> 'Through official secrecy and ridicule, many
> citizens are led to believe that the unknown
> flying objects are nonsense.'
>
> Rear Admiral Hillenkoetter
> Director C.I.A. (1947 - 50)

> 'They are here without a doubt, but
> what they are is anybody's guess.'
>
> Brigadier General and Astronaut
> James McDivett

'There has been contact – period.'

Colonel Gordon Cooper, test pilot, astronaut, and witness to what he also asserts are interplanetary craft. In his book 'Leap of Faith'

Colonel Cooper has put much of the detail before the public with bluntness, clarity and courage in the face of state propaganda and disinformation, and what he has deemed, unnecessary secrecy.

It must be remembered, these are competent military men of high office, entrusted with the security of both Britain and the United States who have made these statements.

The above quotes have been taken from those readily to hand and do confirm what most of the general public of most cultures are open-minded about, namely, that non-earthly, non-manmade craft of stupendous flight parameters are flying in the airspace surrounding the planet and obviously interstellar space. They are piloted by intelligent beings beyond our ken, either within the craft themselves or robotically controlled from distance. Either way non-terrestrial agencies are directly involved.

After the Russian authorities had made lengthy investigations into the strange aerial craft (mainly circular) witnessed in that country during the Cold War period, they also came to the conclusion that they had 'an alien civilisation present.'

And yet, we have had a history of denials and the deliberate suppression of these facts by both the British and American state authorities. The subterfuge, ridicule and disinformation, does suggest a concern that official announcement would be dangerous. Even so, this 'fear of panic in the population' is not borne out by the situation in Mexico.

Throughout the 1990's with little or no reporting in British newsrooms, Mexico City was inundated with sightings. The people themselves were seeing these discs daily, with the Mexican government remaining non-influential. It does invite the question as to what is lacking in Western cultures (or their overseers) that will view the same phenomena with such acute hostility and paranoia.

A prided 'advanced' culture like ours having to be protected from self-evident truths to avoid panic, when a more agrarian society is perfectly at ease with the knowledge of these craft. Undenied by their government and enthusiastic in their reporting, the Mexican media have never been shackled. The reality of these agencies and their craft, as has been substantively reported, is a source of great wonder to the Mexican people. The so-called panic envisaged by Western governments – nonexistent.

From this cultural experience alone, it seems most unlikely that panic would follow official confirmation of these agencies. So the Western peoples are, it would seem, viewed as somewhat fragile of character by their own elected and non-elected officials.

The most recent disinformation to convince that all those innocent and incredulous statements over the past sixty years or so, by various level headed men and women of both the civilian and the military, were all part of a deception plan to hide the truth of secret technology and its development.

Those responsible for military security would not

deliberately station secret aircraft of any sort over Mexico City in full daylight, to be especially viewed by the population at large, and within civilian flight paths. It is both unnecessary and defeats the object of secrecy in the first place, as well as putting civilian populations at serious risk from such experimental craft. It does emphasise however, the continuous need, whether it be right or wrong, to deny the reality of what is related in these final two chapters.

The U2 high flying powered glider and spy plane of the United States Air Force for example, was unknown in civic circles until brought down by the long burn interceptor missiles of Soviet Russia. The futuristic and aesthetically appealing Mach 3 Blackbird SR71 aircraft of the same Air Force had been superseded and was out of commission before the public ever set eyes on it. And apparently not even the management of Lockheed knew of the design and building of the Stealth bomber, the F-117 at their factory, until it was in the air. So secrets can be kept if the need is paramount, even if reasons may vary.

On the other hand it may be true that in the industrialised Western cultures, where agrarian or nomadic interdependence has been lost, the carnal clinging of the conscious mind may have become the price for industrial wealth and political centralisation.

Understandably, we are told that anything that will disturb or panic the collective psyche is outlawed, that is if panic would ensue. Many have greater confidence that the Western populations will not be overwhelmed by the truth of alien reality, abduction or agenda and what is about to happen to the human species. For a beautiful thing it is.

> 'You don't know the half of it'
> George Bush the elder on flying saucer secrecy.

The scenario that has been argued time and again, as reason to retain secrecy, is that should detailed official announcement of these agencies take place, the seeming brittle foundation upon which most governmental institutions are based would likely be shattered. With the bedrock in pieces, the remainder would follow. An unenviable position to be in, for it does appear that our large contemporary communities are dependent upon social structure for their security and comfort, not only of body but also of mind. Boldly announcing the truth on a daily newscast is deemed to be irresponsible. The panic in the population generated by the Orson Wells saga of 1938, may be the defining criteria in the mind of today's policy makers.

The argument continues, that life saving slow infusions of many pints of blood are given daily to patients in hospitals all over the world. A single sudden infusion would send the body into shock and death would follow. The slow seeping of the truth (whether planned or not) of these machines, the beings who fly them and their agenda, into the human psyche, is probably the most sensible thing to do.

It is the experience of very few to retain conscious memory of seeing or even knowing to some degree, these agencies or 'other intelligences.' To the parochial or enfeebled, the psychological shock could possibly lead to mental disorientation or even madness. A dream is one thing, acknowledged reality another.

Even after many years of intellectual appraisal and reappraisal of the phenomena, surprisingly, it still remains momentarily disturbing when the truth of the reality is finally accepted. Why the certainty arrives into one's psyche with such suddenness who can know, but that moment is never forgotten. Those who become aware through actual contact have my deepest sympathy, for the instant destruction of previously held inculcated norms, must generate the most imponderable trauma.

> 'I can assure you that flying saucers, given that they exist, are not constructed by any power on earth.'
>
> President Harry S Truman at a press conference in 1950

A tongue in cheek political pretence about the certainty of their existence is not out of place, but if unaware of their existence how could President Truman know they were not constructed on earth.

Although deliberately stationing themselves over Mexico City to be viewed by an incredulous population, it does appear in general that these alien agencies are reluctant to make direct contact with large numbers of the civilian population. Their social non-attachment is understandable when their primary purpose is the complex genetic modification that they have been under obligation to complete.

The obtaining of spermatozoa, ova and anything else they would have needed, through the controlling public institutions of human governments would have inevitably proved impossible. They have had no choice but to respond to the human call, and no choice but to keep their programme of genetic 'hybridisation' to themselves, which in turn, means their own identity as well.

If it is an impossible task to considerably improve the trivial, the game of international soccer for instance, by altering the 1866 offside rule to mirror that of ice-hockey, and avoid the debacle of twenty super-fit young men crashing around in a narrow central area of the field, then what we are talking about here wouldn't even get a slant-eyed glance let alone a green paper or an active participation within the bodies of institution.

It is obvious that these craft are of the solid, yet it seems they have a capacity to somehow 'reconstruct' time and space around themselves, which may be their means of propulsion or travel.

We are told that no lightweight element exists on planet earth which would protect protoplasm from the deadly effect of the Van Allen radiation belts or fast travelling bullet like meteorites, or the winds of intense radiation expelled from the surface of the sun into interstellar space. Ten foot thick lead screening being out of the question.

Ultimately this would mean that mammalian life is

imprisoned on this planet or at least underneath the Van Allen radiation belts, unless of course, material is imported from somewhere else in the universe, or the space capsule can generate, its own effective electromagnetic radiation shield. Neither shield nor lightweight material were available back in the 1960's and 70's and possibly not even available today.

This is one reason why it must be supposed claims are made that the moon landings were falsified. It has to be admitted that many of the stills and some video relating to the landings have been manufactured on earth, for public relation purposes no doubt. A sort of 'sanitised television style makeover.'

More embarrassing than the earth created images, has been the visible discomfort of honest men attempting to defend those images of the Apollo landings.

Contemporary investigators fail to realise or don't wish to know that the Western world was at the time, in one huge political arm wrestle, and seeking to sabotage the incarcerating ambitions of ruthless dictators. I well remember a Russian KGB member in studio discussion in Britain in the 1950's barking at one student who was asking penetrating questions of enforced socialism,

> 'you can only speak to me as you do because you live in this country. You wouldn't do so if you were in my country.'

We of the Western world owe a debt of gratitude to many unknown, unselfish and unheralded men and women who, as those who lived through it well know, promoted the freedom of men everywhere. In those days, not so long ago the international stakes could not have been higher.

Astronaut and scientist Mr. Edgar Mitchell explained in 1998, that immediately after landing on the moon in Apollo 14, he had the deep feeling that the universe and all life form is 'of one giant consciousness.' No man could be witness to such truth and then deceive millions upon millions of people.

We should also be honest with ourselves and admit it is quite our human nature to initially be repulsed by that which is different. What could be more different than creatures, albeit benign, from another planet, another space, time or dimension. Even though we can adjust quite quickly, all species need self assurance. Could it really be possible that such contact would lead to physical indolence, psychological lethargy or apathy on a massive scale. Presently these alien agencies, it seems, have no wish to communicate with us on a physical level, for if that was their wish, they could do so quite easily, at any time.

Is it any wonder that as their existence has seeped into the collective consciousness, 'they are coming to eat you' stories abound. From the soul stealing, bug-eyed pygmy-sized biped, to the grotesque nine foot tall upright rapacious reptile.

The succession to the Homo sapiens species, revealed by government or alien agency, may be too shocking for many to contemplate; revealed by a layman continues the slow soft drip or seeping of information. It appears the need to feed this information of succession into the public domain has to be from the bottom rung of the social ladder – upwards, as has historically been the case with other truths. A narrative speaks to an individual, governments address a people.

The silver discs and glowing orbs, Mr. Yung tells us, could be psychological projections or 'visionary rumours,' themselves the result of emotional tensions. This comes very close indeed to the 'press' that has been reiterated in previous pages.

It is now obvious, as regards to these flying discs and their occupants, that mental and emotional imaginings are not the actual fact. These craft are solid, with solid intelligent beings navigating them, well within the definition of solid matter as we understand it. Not called into being by us, but called towards us, not a psychological imagining but a response to that human call.

Often in a sitting room full of house plants, as you walk through, one will draw your attention, attract you to it, call out to you as it were. Invariably the pot is light, the plant needs water. It may sound extraordinary in this our mechanistic culture, and to some no doubt, a nonsense, but it is true. How it all works can anyone ever be sure, but work it does. So it seems to be, with those who have heard our call of distress.

As a somewhat dark and to my mind mistaken conclusion regarding this alien agency intervention, Mr.

Yung in his book 'Flying Saucers' emphasises,

> 'Consciousness commits the same grave mistake as the insane person: it understands the event as a concrete external happening and not as a subjective symbolic process.'

It must be stated that although the psychological principle is correct in its essence, the application is incorrect as it applies to this phenomenon of visiting alien agencies.

There is now a wealth of conscious space/time experience, multiple and mass sightings, missing abductees, (the truth of their experiences verified by lie detector tests), video and photographic aerial observation and many broken secrets by men at the very heart of Majestic-12. A group of scientific and military personnel, assembled in the 1950's in an attempt to understand the meaning of this extraterrestrial phenomena, and to formulate a policy of secrecy.

There is also a wealth of accumulated knowledge of the physical form of these disc shaped vehicles along with the associated events. Mr. Yung initially, seemed hesitant to accept the accumulating physical knowledge. Silent, apparently weightless objects very easily became weightless thoughts.

We are graphically warned of this trap in the introduction to Mr. Yung's same book 'Flying Saucers,'

> 'the danger that our judgement will remain caught in subjectivity is great.'

Mr. Yung, a confirmed sceptic in those early days, doesn't bring himself to state outright that 'UFO's do not exist,' but uses these same words of Dr. Hugh Dryden and then vigorously agrees with him.

Mr. Yung does state however, (Flying Saucers, page 23) that he was once convinced that nothing heavier than air could fly. Caught in the sticky web of subjectivity, he failed to appreciate that every bird from the prehistoric to the present day, has been and still is, heavier than air. Even so, Mr. Yung had the courage and integrity to admit his gross error.

These other agencies and their nuts and bolts craft, Mr. Yung has stated, are 'human fantasies.' In this instance, it must be said, that he is again in error.

> 'The phenomenon is something real
> and not visionary or fictitious.'
> General N.F. Twining
> Chief of Staff. U.S.A.F. (1955–58)

Eventually, Mr. Yung had to concede that the alien agency craft were real. He later advised that secrecy about this issue was ultimately detrimental to the psychological health of the population in general. Disinformation and orchestrated denial he describes as 'ridiculous antics.' Again his courage self evident.

With all the available information now to hand, those who state there are no alien agencies flying solid craft in the earth's atmosphere, are either employed by one of the various state policy departments, or have an understandable need to retain personal security within the confines of an existing conscious view of a singular reality.

And returning to the quotes at the beginning of this chapter, it also appears that many high placed men of integrity are irritated by all the seeming unnecessary secrecy surrounding this issue. Seeming, because the next question after 'Are they here?' if it be truthfully answered in the affirmative, is 'Why are they here?'

Before entering the final chapter there was one particular incident which is worth repeating, although not quite along the usual extraterrestrial lines.

Having always had a hankering for flying, one determined and adventurous American decided he would inflate some balloons with helium, bought from his local gas store, and tie them to his garden chair. He calculated that after reaching a satisfactory height he could descend by shooting the balloons, one at a time, with a pellet gun he would take with him.

Casting off the tethering weight he ascended rapidly and just as quickly became much too fearful to shoot at the balloons in case his descent became too rapid. An understandable reaction when you have the world at your feet.

Anyway, he was eventually spotted by the pilot of a commercial aircraft who contacted the ground explaining somewhat excitedly, that at eleven thousand feet, he had just passed a man sitting in a garden chair, held aloft by a bevy of balloons, and waving a gun about.

Desperately clinging onto rescuers each side of him, still shaking in terror, faced with massed ranks of TV cameras and forthcoming celebrity, and looking out through semi-transfixed eyes, he was heard to whisper to himself,

"And there was I just hanging around"

CHAPTER TWELVE

WHY ARE THEY HERE?

> 'It is reasonable to believe and affirm that extraterrestrials exist. Their existence can no longer be denied.'
>
> Father Corrado Balducci
> Priest of Honour to the Papacy

As governments and their military are unwilling or unable to reveal the facts of the extraterrestrial presence, it has been left to civilian men and women to attempt to get at the truth themselves. By the civilian exposure of these truths, the hard factuality of an official newscast has been avoided, for while in civilian hands there is always a perceived atmosphere of speculation, in which the uncertain or distressed can find sanctuary. In this respect, the peacetime authorities can be seen as prudent and cautious. To some without civic responsibility, maybe over prudent and over cautious.

With an obvious need to be secretive in their activities, these 'other agencies' are not going to leave physical proof of their comings and goings, so other avenues have been undertaken. One of the most prominent being hypnotic regression, and through it, the retrieval of the astonishing experiences of abductees.

It is inevitable that hypnotic regression, as a means of retrieving forgotten or buried memories of real events, is approached with caution if not on occasions, suspicion. That hypnosis can retrieve forgotten or buried memories, of that there is little doubt, but memories of what is the main question. Not all retrieved memory is false, but a proportion of it is. False in the sense that a particular memory, although vividly real to the hypnotised person, can still be false in reality, well, our reality.

It is also common knowledge that some quite normal people, when placed under hypnosis, for some reason, adopt a different identity or personality to that of their everyday life. It's not clear why this should happen but happen it does.

Of the real memories, of the many hypnotic regression cases of the late Dr. Mack and Dr. David Jacobs, certain experiences occur again and again, primarily abduction itself, the removal of ova and semen, and contact with hybrid beings in various stages of maturity. Because of the independence of these abductees, one to the other, before engaging in the process of hypnosis, the authenticity of these common experiences is persuasive indeed.

However, the lurid details of one or two instances of warring hybrid pilots and bestial behaviour, is more than likely fantasizing. Although the common thread of a genetic programme is clear and incontrovertible, these isolated 'horror memories' are probably instigated in the abductee by the enormity of the trauma suffered from the prolonged fear and terror on the individual human mind, inducing in its turn, a probable if temporary split in personality.

Some abductees, it has to be stated, do show considerable resentment at the way they have been 'used as lab rats.' It is understandable, that in reaction to such feelings of 'rape and abuse' they contend that these agencies are not here to further the spiritual or psychic health of mankind or the development of the species.

While their mental terror may have been overwhelming and their emotional wounds deep indeed, their conclusions are not as many other abductees have come to understand.

Nonetheless, hypnosis is generally accepted as a useful tool especially when as stated, almost identical experiences emerge time after time from independent sources, and confirmed by those who have memory of their own abduction even without having been subjected to hypnosis.

Although appearing detached, respect is shown by these alien agencies for each individual involved. It does seem that the birth pains of a new species are at times unpleasant. It is our sorrows, our inner need and struggle, along with the trauma of abduction that will herald forth the wonder and joy of the Supplant.

Those chosen and directly involved in the birth-pangs of the coming species, should be given every assistance, comfort and help to recover, and not the ostracising many abductees have been subjected to, just because the reality of abduction appears as nought more than wild imaginings to others.

As a child, the white-robed being I witnessed at my bedside, will never be anything but real, even though shocked, in fear, and clinging to mother's hand,

"There is no one here but me," she repeated.

Yet there was, for many minutes it stood at her side, staring and unmoving.

The late Dr. John Mack, a professor of psychiatry at Harvard Medical School, in just three and a half years in the early nineties, worked with over a hundred individuals directly involved in alien abduction, which he stated affected him most profoundly.

When a professional man of this calibre risked aspersion along with multiple and various malevolent accusations, for integrity and honesty sake, then it surely has to be obvious, that forces abound which seek to discredit genuine information and experience, in order to retain a culturally entrenched consensus reality. And also because such information doesn't fit into the present day biologically induced mindset or paradigm.

None should comment, whatever their social status, upon the validity or otherwise of alien abduction and its importance to our immediate future, unless having first studied thoroughly the enormous and important work of Dr. Mack.

'Abduction' written by Dr. Mack, is probably one of the most unbiased and accurate reports of this extraordinary phenomena. The book itself, is an in-depth conveyance of the truth of the alien reality. An often disturbing truth, understandably repressed by both intellectual and military elites, who see not only threat to the predominant materialistic worldview, but also threat to the institutions which support and protect it.

The conclusions of Dr. Mack, that abductions are first and foremost about the 'joining of two species' to produce a broader consciousness of more advanced capability, most readily concur with what I have come to understand, along with the reasoned study of the subject from many different viewpoints and many different sources over the past fifty years or so.

Had this combination of intuitive understanding and reasoned deduction, revealed a parallel or convergence with Mr. Julian Huxley, and his contemporary self-confessed materialists of both the physiological and psychological sciences, then it would only be honest to say so. But they don't. The ground of our being is not the same as the ground of our material awareness.

> 'The world of error is ignorant of the world of truth.'
> Mary Baker Eddy
> Christian Science and Key to the Sciptures

In other words, the physiological consciousness of soil and science, theory and theorem is ignorant of the world of that which is indwelling, and which it concludes must be apparition or some such non-entity. Unfortunately, no amount of qualification can enlighten us, if for example and as suggested earlier, the temporal lobe(s) does not have full function, for it does appear that this is the organ or area of the brain through which intuition becomes manifest.

Much as the plaintive animal, trapped in a crevasse maybe, is hauled free by the ingenuity and compassion of men, so the use of intervening intelligences in the genetic alteration, has produced the physical form of the coming Supplant.

The intelligence, compassion and commitment of something greater than ourselves working for us, whether we know it or not, whether we accept the premise or not.

So we come to what looks like, to outside eyes, a somewhat agricultural way of generating a new species form. That is, the need to abduct and then to directly obtain both spermatozoa and ova for genetic manipulation, while holding the abductees on very advanced space vehicles.

It does appear an unrefined way to go about things, but biological form is just that and DNA as the base building block is common to all sentient life on earth. Even so, the complexity of the DNA manipulation required to produce new but precise species form must have been immense, and it is here that the horrendous burden of confining, dense and sorrowful human incarnation is to end.

Dr. Jacobs, who has also studied abductions in depth, has come to much the same conclusion as Dr. Mack, but expresses his conclusions rather differently, in that he sees the new species to come, as a hybrid takeover of the Earth.

Dr. Jacobs readily states that he approaches the subject from an investigative need, rather than the therapeutic need of Dr. Mack. But, it is the ultimate conclusion of both, that abduction is a reality, and that the extracted semen and ova obtained from abductees is used for genetic engineering. And they also both agree that the resulting 'hybrid' offspring, is about the future of this planet. Dr. Mack seeing an expanded consciousness, Dr. Jacobs seeing a demonic domination,

> 'All their *(alien agencies)* efforts and activities seem to be geared towards complete control of humans on earth.'
>
> Dr. David Jacobs

We cannot help but ask what any advanced agency would want to control the human species for anyway. While we can possibly overstate our own species importance, the control of the human race, or any part of it, is only a degenerating and immature human need; it is hardly likely the need of any other. Their contact with us is but a reaction, and their use of human genetics, is but the use of genetic building blocks.

And, if dominion were part of any alien agency agenda, past or present, then they could have obtained that dominance at any time. They haven't, neither will they.

While Dr. Jacobs in his work 'The Threat' correctly realises the physiological importance and 'usability' of the human genome in the forthcoming biological change, he unfortunately sees sinister intent in the purposes to which that genome has been used.

It does seem that each species is unique in part, and that biological continuity is in some way a necessity.

It is Dr. Jacobs' personal interpretation that this succession is a 'catastrophe' to the Homo sapiens. We have to wonder why such an unfolding biological scenario can be physically demonic to one professional man while being a wondrous spiritual event to another.

Dr. Jacobs doesn't question that the new species has been bred, engineered or brought into existence by outside agencies; his disquiet is that they are coming to conquer. That the destiny of the planet will not be governed by ourselves. That is precisely the point, and as repeated throughout these writings, the call, the need to 'live as soul' has been made from deep within the collective consciousness of the Homo sapiens itself.

A call made generation after generation, either esoterically through, reflection, contemplation and prayer, or less reverentially through vulgarity and curse. A call made of those crushed by fear and hopelessness, mauled by grief and loss, isolated through lives of loneliness and of those sickened by injustice, where might and brute have ruled.

The Supplant cannot forcibly inhabit the planet like some strutting Caesar of antiquity, so the incarceration and inevitable subjugation envisaged by Dr. Jacobs is totally unfounded, in fact impossible.

However, while Dr. Jacobs could be correct in

suggesting 'integration' as an inevitability of succession, his use of the word 'disastrous' is again a personal interpretation indicative of his viewing of this issue from a single point of view, a cognitive view centred within the human species.

From the opinions and conclusions of Dr. Jacobs, there is very little impression that the species Homo sapiens is anything other than the summation of ultimate creation and fashioned with inviolable preservation. Succession is inevitable at some stage in the future whatever the truth or track of biological variation, for even the materialist has decreed,

> 'the evolution of man follows the
> self same path as the animals'

The 'hybrid' – the species to come, is complete, the Homo sapiens to be released into extinction, yet humanity walks on. Through grace, the soul of man incarnating into conditions of its own purer dreaming.

If 'integration' is to happen then an interactive cohabitation of the human and its successor will have to take place, which means that prior to this, it is likely a universal contact and communication will also have to take place.

Although the majority of ordinary folk, possibly after a careful approach, would extend a friendly hand, it has been suggested, that it is not something the unseen men of power would be pleased about. It is a possible, if unlikely reason for all the secrecy, but the main reason does appear to be this fear of social dislocation.

This fear of dislocation must have been a terrible dilemma for the governing authorities of the Western world at least, and highlighted by a situation in 1972 when a certain Mr. Robert Emernacor was given a brief by American military intelligence. His brief was to produce a television documentary actually showing the landing of an extraterrestrial craft and the contact of its occupants with military personnel at the Holloman Air Force base. A contact that took place eight years earlier in 1964.

As with the initial military disclosure and publication of the finding of a damaged flying disc at Roswell in 1947, uncertainty raised its head, and although the film was eventually made, it was made as a possible happening. The actual recording of the landing and contact at the base – shelved, and destined not to be released. Policy within the U.S.A. became one of denial and that is how it has remained ever since.

It is known that studies from the respected 'think tank' – The Brookings Institute, did state that there would be serious social upheaval if it was officially revealed that contact with alien agencies had taken place. And what influence, if any, these extraterrestrial agencies themselves may have had in the adoption of secrecy and denial, few would know anyway.

Communal awareness of the truth of extraterrestrial activity on this planet, says the Institute, would dramatically shift the communal consciousness, with upheavals coming to all institutions, political, economic and religious. To those who have the power to 'retain the status quo at any price' the secular cultural bubble would be burst and into the unknown we would all have to go.

There are of course bound to be some in every generation who would not joyfully herald in the coming collective and its elevated consciousness, and would not welcome the coming of the 'man born anew.' Yet it is something that cannot be stopped, for the call in all its forms, continues to emanate from the heart of man and will do so until the need to 'live as soul,' to live in continuous childlike love of our spiritual Father be fulfilled, not only in the occasional individual but in the species as a whole, where none shall be deficient of such wonder.

It also follows that as a cosmic creature, the ability of the Supplant to protect planet Earth, and all its life forms, becomes infinitely greater. The living breathing planet will have an extended and more protective shield, not only reaching out into deep space, but equally into the finer matter and resonance of a deeper consciousness.

'Oh Lord, when will this beautiful earth be ready to receive thy saints?' pleads the Joan of Bernard Shaw.

The mechanics of the transition and inception of the Supplant onto the earth, of that nothing is known to me. I have asked but have been discouraged, and there it must for me, be left to lie. Maybe in the time between now and then some other soul is destined to release such detail. A soul with its own particular personal strengths and insights.

It would be easy to envisage a gathering of the final apocalyptic remains of a species staring with awe at a booming and swirling multi-coloured stratosphere parting to allow through ghostly forms of haloed ectoplasmic beings.

Earlier commentary tells us this is not going to be. The Supplant is not ectoplasmic but protoplasmic, of biological form, different yet similar to ourselves and coming to earth from the heavens or what is referred to as outer space – beyond earth's atmosphere.

It can only be our ignorance of the incarnating processes that would produce fear of this coming dawn, now almost upon us. And it is now that the whole spectrum of the extraterrestrial phenomena of the past sixty or seventy years begins to take an unmistakable shape. It has been obvious during that period, alien agencies have been at work on this planet. This fact, as already stated, carefully concealed by governments.

Whether or not the true intention of these agencies has been revealed to state authorities, again few would know. And if such knowledge has been given to any military authority, it is understandable they would seek to cloak it behind a veil of secrecy.

It is also apparent that any being or species to come, in its all wise consciousness would be impossible to govern by deceit or clandestine policies, and its all seeing tenderness unresponsive to coercion.

And finally, it must be repeated that the most significant agreement of both Dr. Mack and Dr. Jacobs is that the abductions, the genetic manipulation and its subsequent breeding programme is about this planet, its immediate future and what is to come.

It is my understanding, that what is to come, is a biological creature, yet a cosmic creature, able to traverse the deep reaches of space.

As a living being it cannot bring distress to any life form, is sensitive to all consciousness and fulfils its loving need without dominion. Having mind free to soar the plains and valleys, forest and sea, confident, unfettered and fearless.

Also of a mind with a deep understanding not only of technologies but reality shifts in both space and time, able to understand emanating brain patterns or thought without language or tongue, and similarly, able to convey its ineffable love to each and to all.

A being untroubled by nightmare or threat and in continuous conscious fusion with Cosmic Mind and Love.

‘and there shall be one fold and one shepherd’

Epilogue

With the completion of this writing, a personal obligation has been fulfilled.

Weary as we may become of temporal existence and its attendant biological constriction of consciousness, we must always remember that we ourselves have sought and elected to be born into such conditions.

Grateful in many different ways, it is nonetheless my fervent hope and will be my dieing wish that such temptation will never again befall my spirit.

A gift indeed it would be,
If no mark remain of me.
Make no shrine, pick no flower,
Scatter my ashes I care not where.
Consider not the passing hour
But the coming Supplant heir.

Further Reading

Psychology and the Religious Quest. Prof. R, B. Cattel. *Thomas Nelson. 1938.*

Edgar Cayce on Prophesy. Mary Ellen Carter. *Warner Books. 1968.*

The Cloud of Unknowing. Halcyon Backhouse. *Hodder and Stoughton. 1985.*

Man and his Symbols. Carl Yung. *Picador. 1964.*

The Secret of the Golden Flower. C. G. Yung and R.Wilhelm. *Routledge and Kegan Paul. 1950.*

Forever Ours. Dr. Janis Amatuzio. *Hodder and Stoughton. 2006.*

The Mystery of the Mind. Wilder Penfield. *Princetown University Press. 1975.*

The Conscious Universe. Dean Radin. *HarperEdge. 1997.*

The Devine Vision. Stewart. *M. Houghton. 1939.*

Christian Science and Key to the Scriptures. Mary Baker Eddy. *The First Church of Christ. Cont.*

The Third Mystic. Frances Parkinson Keyes. *Peter Davies. 1960.*

In God's Name. David Yallop. *Transworld Publishers 1986.*

Mystical Life of Jesus. Spencer Lewis. *AMORC. 1966.*

When the Earth Nearly Died. Allan and Delair. *Gateway Books. 1995.*

Further Reading

The Mind of Light. Sri Aurobindo. *Lotus Press. 2003.*
Walk On. Christmas Humphreys. *The Buddhist Society. 1965.*
Leap of Faith. Gordon Cooper. *HarperCollins Publishers. 2000.*
Flying Saucers. Carl Yung. *Routledge and Kegan Paul. 1977.*
Abduction. Prof. John Mack. *Simon and Schuster. 1995.*
The Threat. David Jacobs. *Simon and Schuster. 1998.*

The author. (2011)